A READING GUIDE TO THE DOCTRINE AND COVENANTS

DAVID H. MULHOLLAND

Deseret Book Company
Salt Lake City, Utah

To David, John, Brian, Sarah, Roger, and Matthew

ISBN 0-87579-182-4

Printed in the United States of America

10 9 8 7 6 5 4 3 2

Contents

Preface

This guide will help you better understand the revelations contained in the Doctrine and Covenants and Joseph Smith's own story, which is recorded in Joseph Smith–History. As this guide helps you focus on the important principles contained in these modern-day scriptures, your testimony of the truths you study will be strengthened and you will be motivated to apply them in your life.

President Ezra Taft Benson has reminded us that "the Doctrine and Covenants is the binding link between the Book of Mormon and the continuing work of the Restoration through the Prophet Joseph Smith and his successors.

"In the Doctrine and Covenants we learn of temple work, eternal families, the degrees of glory, Church organization, and many other great truths of the Restoration.

" 'Search these commandments,' said the Lord of the Doctrine and Covenants, 'for they are true and faithful, and the prophecies and promises which are in them shall all be fulfilled.

" 'What I the Lord have spoken, I have spoken, and I excuse not myself; and though the heavens and the earth pass away, my word shall not pass away, but shall all be fulfilled, whether by mine own voice or by the voice of my servants, it is the same' (D&C 1:37–38).

"The Book of Mormon brings men to Christ. The Doctrine and Covenants brings men to Christ's kingdom, even The Church of Jesus Christ of Latter-day Saints, 'the only true and living church upon the face of the whole earth' (v. 30). I know that.

"The Book of Mormon is the 'keystone' of our religion, and the Doctrine and Covenants is the capstone, with continuing latter-day revelation. The Lord has placed His stamp of approval on both the keystone and the capstone." (*Ensign,* May 1987, p. 83.)

My thanks to—

My wife, Lois, and our children for allowing me the time necessary to write and for their helpful suggestions

Allen Fletcher and Dennis Lifferth for their thoughtful review and helpful suggestions

Eleanor Knowles and Suzanne Brady, both of Deseret Book, for their assistance in transforming the manuscript into a finished book

How to Use This Reading Guide

When you begin your study of the Doctrine and Covenants, first read the section in the scriptures before you answer the questions in the guide.

Next, go back through the section you have just read, and write in the guide the answer and the number of the verse or verses where the answer is found. (You will find most of the answers in the section you are reading in the Doctrine and Covenants, but you will need to look for a few answers in other places in the scriptures.)

Then compare the verse or verses you wrote down with the verses listed in the Answers section at the back of this guide.

Review the answers from your last study session before you go on. Discussing with others what you have studied will also help you remember what you have learned.

The designation "See" after a question refers you to the passage where you will find the answer. This designation is used only when the answer is not in the section you are currently reading. For example, "See D&C 1:16*a*" means that you will find all or part of the answer in footnote *a* to verse 16 of Doctrine and Covenants 1.

The designation "See also" refers you to related information that is not necessarily part of the answer. For example, you may be referred to the Bible Dictionary, which is in the appendix to the Latter-day Saint edition of the King James Version of the Bible.

Questions without a letter designation are thought questions to help you "liken unto yourself" the principles you are studying.

In addition to the scriptures and this guide, the following books will help you better understand the history and doctrine you are reading:

The Doctrine and Covenants Commentary, by Hyrum M. Smith and Janne M. Sjodahl. Revised edition published by Deseret Book Company, 1978.

The Revelations of the Prophet Joseph Smith: A Historical and Biographical Commentary of the Doctrine and Covenants, by Lyndon W. Cook. Published by Deseret Book Company, 1985.

The Doctrine and Covenants Student Manual, prepared by the Church Educational System and published by The Church of Jesus Christ of Latter-day Saints, 1981.

Following is a brief outline of some of the events in Church history that are related to your study of the Doctrine and Covenants:

December 1805	Joseph Smith, Jr., is born. (See Joseph Smith–History.)
Spring 1820	Joseph has his first vision. (See Joseph Smith–History.)
September 1823	Joseph is visited by Moroni and told of the gold plates. (See Joseph Smith–History.)
September 1827	Joseph receives the plates. (See Joseph Smith–History.)
July 1828	Joseph learns that Martin Harris has lost 116 pages of manuscript. (See D&C 3.)
May 1829	The Aaronic Priesthood is restored by John the Baptist. (See D&C 13.)
May 1829	Oliver Cowdery and Joseph are baptized. (See Joseph Smith–History.)
June 1829	The Melchizedek Priesthood is restored by Peter, James, and John. (See D&C 13.)
March 1830	The Book of Mormon is published. (See D&C 19.)
April 1830	The Church is organized. (See D&C 21.)
July 1830	Emma Smith is asked to make a selection of sacred hymns. (See D&C 25.)
December 1830	The Saints are instructed to move to Ohio because of persecution. (See D&C 37.)

February 1831	Edward Partridge is ordained the first bishop. (See D&C 41.)
August 1831	Independence, Missouri, is designated to be the city of Zion. (See D&C 57.)
February 1832	The revelation on the degrees of glory is received. (See D&C 76.)
September 1832	The revelation on priesthood is received. (See D&C 84.)
December 1832	The Lord commands the Saints to build a temple in Kirtland, Ohio. (See D&C 88.)
July 1833	The Saints are forced to agree to leave Jackson County, Missouri. (See D&C 97.)
April 1834	The united order is temporarily dissolved. (See D&C 104.)
June 1834	Zion's camp is disbanded. (See D&C 105.)
January 1836	Joseph sees in vision his mother and father and brother Alvin in the celestial kingdom. (See D&C 137.)
March 1836	The Kirtland Temple is dedicated. (See D&C 109.)
July 1837	The gospel is first preached in England. (See D&C 112.)
July 1838	The law of tithing is received. (See D&C 119.)
October 1838	The exterminating order is issued by Governor Boggs of Missouri. (See D&C 124.)
July 1839	Joseph Smith is incarcerated in Liberty Jail in Missouri. (See D&C 121.)
January 1841	The Saints are commanded to build a temple in Nauvoo. (See D&C 124.)
June 1844	Joseph and Hyrum Smith are killed in Carthage, Illinois. (See D&C 135.)

January 1847	President Brigham Young receives the pattern for organizing the Saints for their westward trek. (See D&C 136.)
July 1847	The Saints enter the Salt Lake Valley.
October 1890	The Manifesto prohibiting plural marriage in the Church was accepted by the Church as "authoritative and binding." (See Official Declaration–1.)
October 1918	President Joseph F. Smith receives the vision of the redemption of the dead. (See D&C 138.)
June 1978	President Spencer W. Kimball receives the revelation extending priesthood and temple blessings to all worthy male members of the Church. (See Official Declaration–2.)

Explanatory Introduction

PARAGRAPH

________ a. What is the Doctrine and Covenants?

________ b. List two reasons why the Lord speaks to all people.

________ c. What makes the Doctrine and Covenants unique?

________ d. What was Joseph Smith told in his first vision? (See also Joseph Smith–History 1:11–20.)

________ e. What authority did the Church have when it was organized in 1830? (See also Joseph Smith–History 1:1–75.)

________ f. List four things that may be seen in the revelations recorded in the Doctrine and Covenants.

________ g. List twelve fundamental doctrines of the gospel that are explained in the revelations.

________ h. What makes the Doctrine and Covenants "of more worth than the riches of the whole earth"?

________ i. What was the testimony of the Twelve Apostles concerning the revelations?

________ j. What is the process for adding further revelations to the Doctrine and Covenants?

________ k. What are some features of the 1981 edition of the Doctrine and Covenants?

Chronological Order of Contents

PAGE

________ a. Which sections of the Doctrine and Covenants were received before the month in which the Church was organized?

________ b. Where and when was the revelation received that is now recorded in Doctrine and Covenants 1?

________ c. What section of the Doctrine and Covenants was received in Salt Lake City, Utah, in October 1918?

________ d. Where and when was Official Declaration–1 received? Official Declaration–2?

________ e. How many sections of the Doctrine and Covenants contain revelations received from 1830 through 1833?

Doctrine and Covenants 1

VERSE NUMBER

________ a. What was one of the "principal subjects passed upon at the conference"?

________ b. What is Doctrine and Covenants 1?

________ c. To whom is the Lord speaking?

________ d. Why will the rebellious be pierced with much sorrow?

________ e. Who will deliver the warning to all of the people?

________ f. What do they do who "seek not the Lord to establish his righteousness"?

________ g. List three reasons why God called Joseph Smith and others.

________ h. Why did the Lord give these commandments to his servants? (See also Ether 12:27.)

________ i. What will happen to those who will not repent?

________ j. When peace is taken from the earth, what power will the devil have? What power will the Lord have?

________ k. Why should the commandments in the Doctrine and Covenants be searched?

________ l. Why should the voice of the Lord's servants be obeyed?

Doctrine and Covenants 2

VERSE NUMBER

________ a. Which prophet was Moroni quoting to Joseph Smith? (See Joseph Smith–History 1:36–39.)

________ b. What would Elijah the prophet do before the Lord comes? (See also D&C 110:13–16; Bible Dictionary, p. 664, s.v. "Elijah.")

________ c. What would have happened if Elijah had not come to restore the sealing power?

Doctrine and Covenants 3

VERSE NUMBER

________ a. What had the Prophet Joseph Smith given to Martin Harris?

________ b. Why may a man fall even though he has had "many revelations, and [has] power to do many mighty works"?

________ c. What would the Lord have done for Joseph if he had been faithful?

________ d. What did the Lord say would happen to Joseph if he repented? What would happen if he did not repent?

________ e. Why had Joseph lost the privilege to translate?

________ f. List four reasons why the Lord preserved the plates containing the record of the Lamanites and Nephites.

Doctrine and Covenants 4

VERSE NUMBER

________ a. To whom was given the revelation now recorded in Doctrine and Covenants 4?

________ b. What was about to come forth among the children of men?

________ c. How is God to be served, "that ye may stand blameless before [him] at the last day"?

________ d. Who is called to the Lord's work?

________ e. What qualifies a person for the work?

________ f. What should we remember while we are in the service of God?

Doctrine and Covenants 5

VERSE NUMBER

________ a. Who requested the revelation now recorded in Doctrine and Covenants 5?

________ b. What was the first gift bestowed upon Joseph Smith?

________ c. What would Joseph be ordained to do after he translated the plates?

________ d. What power would God give the Three Witnesses?

________ e. What will the Lord do if the inhabitants of the earth do not repent?

________ f. What was required of Joseph to obtain eternal life?

________ g. What did the Lord tell Joseph to say to Martin Harris?

________ h. What was Martin to say in his testimony?

________ i. What was Martin to do in order to see the plates?

_________ j. Why did the Lord tell Joseph to stop translating for a while?

Doctrine and Covenants 6

VERSE NUMBER

_________ a. What had Oliver Cowdery received when the revelation now recorded in Doctrine and Covenants 6 was given?

_________ b. Why should we work with all our might in the service of God?

_________ c. Why is it important to seek for wisdom?

_________ d. What did Oliver need to do to be blessed?

_________ e. What was Oliver's gift? (See Doctrine and Covenants 8:2–5.)

_________ f. What was Oliver to do with his gift?

_________ g. Why had Oliver been able to get to his current place?

_________ h. Why had the Lord told these things to Oliver?

_________ i. What was to be Oliver's relationship with Joseph?

_________ j. What further witness did the Lord give Oliver?

_________ k. What gift did the Lord bestow upon Oliver?

_________ l. Why should we "fear not to do good"?

Doctrine and Covenants 7

VERSE NUMBER

_________ a. Why did Joseph and Oliver inquire of the Lord through the Urim and Thummim?

_________ b. What was the revelation recorded in Doctrine and Covenants 7 translated from?

_________ c. What did the Lord grant unto John? (See also Bible Dictionary, p. 715, s.v. "John.")

_________ d. To whom did the Lord give the keys of the ministry?

Doctrine and Covenants 8

VERSE NUMBER

_________ a. What did Oliver Cowdery desire?

_________ b. How does the Lord reveal things?

_________ c. How was the gift of revelation to protect Oliver?

_________ d. What can we do without faith?

_________ e. What was Oliver to ask for?

Doctrine and Covenants 9

VERSE NUMBER

_________ a. To whom was given the revelation now recorded in Doctrine and Covenants 9?

_________ b. What work was Oliver called to do?

_________ c. What must we do before taking a question before the Lord?

_________ d. How will the Lord answer if it is right? If it is not right?

_________ e. What did the Lord counsel Oliver to do?

What important decision do you need to make in your life? How can you make this decision correctly?

Doctrine and Covenants 10

VERSE NUMBER

_________ a. When was the revelation now recorded in Doctrine and Covenants 10 given to Joseph Smith?

_________ b. What happened to Joseph when he did not obey the Lord?

_________ c. What did the Lord call Martin Harris?

_________ d. Why was Martin called that? (See also D&C 3:12–13.)

_________ e. How should we work in the Church?

_________ f. Why was Joseph to pray always?

_________ g. What was Satan's plan for the lost manuscript?

_________ h. Why does Satan stir up the people?

_________ i. How does the devil flatter the people?

_________ j. Why was Joseph not to show his revelations to the world?

_________ k. What was in the lost manuscript?

_________ l. What is contained in the remainder of the record that Joseph was to translate?

_________ m. What was the faith of the Nephite prophets?

_________ n. Who will the Lord cause to tremble and shake to the center?

_________ o. What is Satan doing to the hearts of the people?

_________ p. Who will the Lord establish upon his rock?

Doctrine and Covenants 11

VERSE NUMBER

_________ a. To whom was given the revelation recorded in Doctrine and Covenants 11?

_________ b. What will happen to those who ask and knock?

_________ c. In verses 6 through 9, what was Hyrum Smith instructed to do?

_________ d. In whom was Hyrum to put his trust?

_________ e. Why was Hyrum commanded not to preach until he was called?

________ f. What was Hyrum (and all other missionaries; see v. 27) to do before preaching the gospel?

________ g. What power will be given to those who receive the Lord?

Doctrine and Covenants 12

VERSE NUMBER

________ a. What had Joseph Knight given to Joseph Smith and Oliver Cowdery?

________ b. What did the Lord say to Joseph Knight and "all those who have desires to bring forth and establish this work"?

________ c. What is required of someone who wants "to assist in this work"?

Doctrine and Covenants 13

VERSE NUMBER

________ a. Who ordained Joseph Smith and Oliver Cowdery to the Aaronic Priesthood? (See also Bible Dictionary, p. 714, s.v. "John the Baptist.")

________ b. Under whose direction was John the Baptist acting?

________ c. What promise was given to Joseph and Oliver?

________ d. What keys are held by the Aaronic Priesthood? (See also Bible Dictionary, p. 599, s.v. "Aaronic Priesthood.")

________ e. What is one reason why the Aaronic Priesthood was restored? (See D&C 13:1*a*; Joseph Smith–History 1:70–72.)

Doctrine and Covenants 14

VERSE NUMBER

________ a. To whom was given the revelation now recorded in Doctrine and Covenants 14?

________ b. Where was the translation of the Book of Mormon completed?

________ c. Which gift is "the greatest of all the gifts of God"?

________ d. What was required for David Whitmer to receive the Holy Ghost?

________ e. How would the Holy Ghost help David?

________ f. What blessing would David receive if he was faithful?

Doctrine and Covenants 15

VERSE NUMBER

________ a. To whom was given the revelation recorded in Doctrine and Covenants 15?

________ b. Why is this revelation personal?

________ c. What had John Whitmer desired of the Lord?

________ d. What did the Lord tell John to do? Why?

Doctrine and Covenants 16

VERSE NUMBER

________ a. To whom was given the revelation recorded in Doctrine and Covenants 16?

________ b. What did Peter Whitmer later become?

________ c. What had Peter desired of the Lord?

________ d. What did the Lord tell Peter to do? Why?

What message do you think the Lord would give to you? (See your patriarchal blessing, if you have one.)

Doctrine and Covenants 17

VERSE NUMBER

________ a. To whom was given the revelation recorded in Doctrine and Covenants 17? Why?

________ b. List five things the Three Witnesses would view if they relied upon the Lord's word "with full purpose of heart."

________ c. How were they to "obtain a view of them"?

________ d. What were they to testify of? Why?

________ e. What did the Lord say about Joseph's translation of the Book of Mormon?

________ f. What would happen if they were faithful in their testimony of the Book of Mormon?

Doctrine and Covenants 18

VERSE NUMBER

________ a. Why was the revelation recorded in Doctrine and Covenants 18 given?

________ b. How did Oliver Cowdery know that the things he had written were true? (See also D&C 9:4.)

________ c. What did the Lord command Oliver to do? Why?

________ d. What should be remembered about the worth of souls?

________ e. Why were Oliver Cowdery and David Whitmer called to "cry repentance unto this people"?

________ f. What will bring us great joy in the kingdom of the Father? What will bring us even greater joy?

________ g. What is the only "name given whereby man can be saved"?

________ h. What did Jesus say to the Twelve Apostles?

________ i. How were David and Oliver to know the Twelve when they found them?

________ j. What is the "marvelous work among the children of men"?

List the names of people you would like to see become members of the Church. List three things you can do to influence them toward baptism. Ask the Lord which of them you should focus your missionary efforts on.

Doctrine and Covenants 19

VERSE NUMBER

________ a. How long before the Church was organized was the revelation received that is recorded in Doctrine and Covenants 19? (See also D&C 21 headnote.)

________ b. To whom was this revelation given?

________ c. Why did the Lord fulfill the will of the Father?

________ d. Why did the Lord suffer in the flesh?

________ e. What will happen to those who do not repent?

________ f. How great was the Lord's suffering for the sins of the world? (See Bible Dictionary, p. 651, s.v. "Crucifixion.")

________ g. To which people was the Book of Mormon soon to go?

________ h. What would happen if Martin Harris "slight[ed] these counsels"?

________ i. What debt was Martin to pay? (See D&C 19:35*b*.)

________ j. Why should Martin pray always?

What sins must you repent of so you will not have to suffer even as Jesus suffered on the cross? (See vv. 13–20.)

Doctrine and Covenants 20

VERSE NUMBER

________ a. What is the theme of the revelation recorded in Doctrine and Covenants 20?

________ b. Upon what day was the Lord's church to be organized? (See also Bible Dictionary, p. 645, s.v. "Church.")

________ c. What is the name of the angel described in Doctrine and Covenants 20:6? (See Joseph Smith–History 1:33; see also D&C 1:6*b*.)

_________ d. What does the Book of Mormon and its witnesses prove to the world?

_________ e. Who will receive a crown of eternal life?

_________ f. From verses 17 through 36 of Doctrine and Covenants 20, list fourteen truths that we learn from the Book of Mormon.

_________ g. How do we become justified and sanctified? (See Moses 6:60.)

_________ h. List the qualifications for those desiring to be baptized.

_________ i. What are the duties of an elder, as stated in verses 38 through 45 of Doctrine and Covenants 20?

_________ j. What are the duties of a priest, as stated in verses 46 through 52?

_________ k. What are the duties of a teacher, as stated in verses 53 through 59?

_________ l. What must be done before a person can be ordained to any office in the Church where there is an organized branch (or ward)?

_________ m. What is required of every Church member who has children?

_________ n. What instructions has the Lord given concerning baptism?

_________ o. Why are members of the Church to meet together often and partake of the sacrament?

_________ p. Why do we partake of the sacramental bread?

_________ q. What will the Father do for those who keep this covenant?

_________ r. Why do we drink the sacramental water?

_________ s. What will the Father do for those who keep this covenant?

Doctrine and Covenants 21

VERSE NUMBER

_________ a. When and where did Joseph Smith receive the revelation recorded in Doctrine and Covenants 21?

_________ b. What was Joseph to be called in the records of the Church?

_________ c. When was the Church organized and established?

_________ d. Why should the prophet be obeyed?

_________ e. What did the Lord inspire Joseph to do?

_________ f. How was Joseph able to claim the powers of heaven?

_________ g. What does the Comforter manifest?

What is your attitude toward the President of the Church when he speaks? (See v. 5.)

Doctrine and Covenants 22

VERSE NUMBER

_________ a. Why did the Lord give the revelation that is now recorded in Doctrine and Covenants 22?

_________ b. What were those who had previously been baptized commanded to do?

Doctrine and Covenants 23

VERSE NUMBER

_________ a. Why was the revelation now recorded in Doctrine and Covenants 23 given?

_________ b. Why was Oliver Cowdery to "beware of pride"?

_________ c. What was Oliver to do?

_________ d. What was Hyrum Smith to do?

_________ e. What was Samuel Smith to do?

_________ f. What was Joseph Smith to do?

_________ g. What was Joseph Knight to do?

Doctrine and Covenants 24

VERSE NUMBER

_________ a. Why did the Church leaders seek safety?

_________ b. What did the Lord do for Joseph Smith?

_________ c. What was Joseph to continue to do?

_________ d. What would be given to Joseph "in the very moment"?

_________ e. What did the Lord tell Joseph about his afflictions?

_________ f. How would Oliver receive "strength such as is not known among men"?

_________ g. Why was Joseph not to worry about the physical necessities of life?

Doctrine and Covenants 25

VERSE NUMBER

_________ a. To whom was given the revelation recorded in Doctrine and Covenants 25?

_________ b. How would Emma Smith be blessed if she was faithful?

_________ c. To what office was Emma called?

_________ d. What should Emma do with her time?

________ e. What was Emma to collect? Why?

________ f. What will the Lord do for those who sing the hymns?

________ g. Why must we keep the commandments?

Doctrine and Covenants 26

VERSE NUMBER

________ a. Why was the revelation received that is recorded in Doctrine and Covenants 26? (See D&C 24 headnote.)

________ b. List four things the Lord told the brethren to do with their time.

________ c. How are all things to be done in the Church?

Doctrine and Covenants 27

VERSE NUMBER

________ a. Under what circumstances was the revelation given that is recorded in Doctrine and Covenants 27?

________ b. Why may we use water instead of wine for the sacrament?

________ c. What does the Lord require of those who partake of the sacrament?

________ d. What keys did the Lord commit to Moroni?

________ e. List eleven prophets the Lord will meet with on the earth.

__________ f. Who is Michael? (See also Bible Dictionary, p. 732, s.v. "Michael".)

__________ g. Who ordained and confirmed Joseph Smith to be an apostle? (See also Bible Dictionary, p. 612, s.v. "Apostle.")

__________ h. Why should we take upon us the whole armor of God?

__________ i. Describe the armor of the Lord.

Doctrine and Covenants 28

VERSE NUMBER

__________ a. What did the professed revelations of Hiram Page concern?

__________ b. Who was the only one appointed to receive revelations and commandments in the Church? (See Bible Dictionary, p. 762, s.v. "Revelation.")

__________ c. In verse 3 of Doctrine and Covenants 28, what was Oliver Cowdery instructed to do?

__________ d. Where will the city of Zion be built? (See D&C 57:2–3.)

__________ e. How was Oliver to correct Hiram Page? (See also D&C 42:88.)

__________ f. Who would tell Oliver what to do on his mission to the Lamanites? (See D&C 28:15*a*.)

Doctrine and Covenants 29

VERSE NUMBER

__________ a. Who was present when the revelation recorded in Doctrine and Covenants 29 was received?

__________ b. Who will be gathered by the Lord?

__________ c. Who are the Lord's elect?

__________ d. Why will they be gathered?

__________ e. What will the Lord do to the wicked?

_________ f. How long will the Lord dwell in righteousness upon the earth?

_________ g. Who will the Lord's twelve apostles from Jerusalem judge?

_________ h. What will happen when the trump in verse 13 shall sound?

_________ i. List seven things that will occur before the second coming of the Lord.

_________ j. What will happen after the thousand years of peace?

_________ k. How does the Lord view and comprehend all things?

_________ l. Why is the devil allowed to tempt us?

_________ m. How did Adam become subject to the will of the devil?

_________ n. How did Adam become spiritually dead?

_________ o. Why did the Lord give Adam and all people a time to repent and prepare to meet Him? (See also Alma 34:33–36.)

_________ p. What will happen to those who do not believe? Why? (See also Bible Dictionary, p. 652, s.v. "Damnation.")

_________ q. Why are children unable to sin before they are eight years old?

Doctrine and Covenants 30

VERSE NUMBER

_________ a. To whom was given the revelation recorded in Doctrine and Covenants 30?

_________ b. What had David Whitmer done to displease the Lord?

_________ c. What was David instructed to do?

_________ d. What was Peter Whitmer instructed to do?

______ e. Who was given power to build up the Church among the Lamanites?

______ f. What was John Whitmer instructed to do?

Doctrine and Covenants 31

VERSE NUMBER

______ a. To whom was given the revelation recorded in Doctrine and Covenants 31?

______ b. How would the Lord bless the family of Thomas B. Marsh?

______ c. How would the Lord bless Thomas on his mission?

______ d. List four things from verse 9 that the Lord counseled Thomas to do.

______ e. How was Thomas to know what to do and where to go?

______ f. Why was Thomas to pray always?

Doctrine and Covenants 32

VERSE NUMBER

______ a. Why was the revelation recorded in Doctrine and Covenants 32 requested?

______ b. What was Parley P. Pratt to do?

______ c. To what were Parley P. Pratt and Ziba Peterson to "give heed to"?

______ d. Why were they to "pray always"?

Doctrine and Covenants 33

VERSE NUMBER

______ a. To whom was given the revelation recorded in Doctrine and Covenants 33?

______ b. What were Ezra Thayre and Northrop Sweet called to do?

______ c. Why do those who do good "err in many instances"? (See also 2 Nephi 26:29.)

______ d. Who will the Lord gather "from the four quarters of the earth"?

______ e. What message were Ezra and Northrop to deliver?

______ f. Why has the Lord given us the scriptures?

Doctrine and Covenants 34

VERSE NUMBER

______ a. How old was Orson Pratt when the revelation recorded in Doctrine and Covenants 34 was received?

______ b. In what two ways was Orson blessed?

______ c. What did the Lord say would soon happen?

______ d. What will happen "before that great day shall come"?

______ e. By what power was Orson to prophesy?

Doctrine and Covenants 35

VERSE NUMBER

______ a. To whom was given the revelation recorded in Doctrine and Covenants 35?

______ b. What was Joseph Smith doing when this revelation was received? (See also Bible Dictionary, p. 717, s.v. "Joseph Smith Translation.")

______ c. For whose sins was Christ crucified?

______ d. In verse 6 of Doctrine and Covenants 35, what was Sidney Rigdon commanded to do?

______ e. What will the Lord do for those who ask in his name and in faith?

______ f. Who are the only ones who are doing good?

_________ g. What had the Lord given to Joseph?

_________ h. In verse 20, what was Sidney commanded to do? (See also headnote.)

_________ i. What would the Lord do if Sidney kept all his covenants?

Doctrine and Covenants 36

VERSE NUMBER

_________ a. To whom and when was the revelation recorded in Doctrine and Covenants 36 given?

_________ b. From verse 1, list three things that Edward Partridge learned.

_________ c. What would the Holy Ghost teach Edward?

_________ d. What calling and commandment was given to Edward concerning all men?

Doctrine and Covenants 37

VERSE NUMBER

_________ a. To whom and when was the revelation recorded in Doctrine and Covenants 37 given?

_________ b. Why were Joseph Smith and Sidney Rigdon to stop translating the Bible? (See also v. 1*a*.)

_________ c. Why were Joseph and Sidney especially to strengthen the Church in Colesville?

_________ d. Where were the Saints to gather? (See v. 3*a*; see also Map, p. 296.)

Doctrine and Covenants 38

VERSE NUMBER

_________ a. At what event was the revelation recorded in Doctrine and Covenants 38 given?

_________ b. For whom has the Lord declared a triple woe? (See 2 Nephi 28:15.)

_________ c. Who will welcome the coming of the Lord?

_________ d. What has caused "silence to reign, and all eternity [to be] pained"?

_________ e. What covenant did the Lord make with the Saints?

_________ f. What is required for people to be "free"?

_________ g. How are we to deal with our brother?

_________ h. What was the mystery that was had "in secret chambers"? (See v. 13.)

_________ i. Why did the Lord tell the Saints these things?

_________ j. Why were the Saints to go to Ohio?

_________ k. How were the Saints to deal with the poor?

_________ l. What were the Saints to beware of?

_________ m. How should we keep the Lord's commandments?

_________ n. How are our neighbors to be warned?

Doctrine and Covenants 39

VERSE NUMBER

_________ a. What covenant had James Covill made with the Lord?

_________ b. Who are they who receive the Lord?

_________ c. What is the Lord's gospel? (See also 3 Nephi 11:31–39; 27:13–21.)

_________ d. Why had James rejected the Lord in the past?

_________ e. How was James to receive the greatest blessing he had ever known?

_________ f. What blessing was to be received in Ohio? (See D&C 95:8–9; 110:8–10; see also 39:15*a*;)

_________ g. For what reason will the Lord "stay [his] hand in judgment"?

________ h. Who will be looking for the Second Coming and know the Lord when he comes?

Doctrine and Covenants 40

VERSE NUMBER

________ a. What had James Covill done?

________ b. How did James Covill receive Doctrine and Covenants 39?

________ c. Why did he reject the word of God?

Doctrine and Covenants 41

VERSE NUMBER

________ a. What were the Church members striving to do?

________ b. Why was the revelation given that is recorded in Doctrine and Covenants 41?

________ c. Who will receive the heaviest of all cursings?

________ d. What were the elders of the Church commanded to do?

________ e. How were the elders to obtain the Lord's law? Why?

________ f. Who is the Lord's disciple?

________ g. To what office was Edward Partridge to be ordained?

________ h. Why was Edward like Nathanael of old? (See also v. 11*a*.)

Doctrine and Covenants 42

VERSE NUMBER

________ a. What promise was fulfilled by the revelation recorded in Doctrine and Covenants 42?

________ b. Why were the elders able to receive this law?

________ c. How were the elders to perform their missions?

________ d. List two things that are required to preach the gospel.

________ e. How is the Spirit obtained?

________ f. What will happen to those who kill?

________ g. List four offenses for which a Church member may be excommunicated if he or she does not repent.

________ h. How should we speak of our neighbor?

________ i. What should we do about the poor?

________ j. What were the Saints to do with their surplus property after the first consecration?

________ k. Why should we not be idle?

________ l. What will happen to those who die in the Lord (endure to the end)?

________ m. What is required for a person to be healed?

________ n. How are the bishop over the storehouse and his counselors to be supported?

________ o. What are all the members of the Church required to do?

________ p. Who are to be delivered up to the law of the land?

________ q. What are we to do with those Church members who have offended us?

________ r. What is to happen to those who "offend openly"?

How can you use the principle given in verse 88 to be reconciled to someone who has offended you?

Doctrine and Covenants 43

VERSE NUMBER

________ a. What concerned some of the Church members?

_________ b. What are the two parts of the revelation recorded in Doctrine and Covenants 43?

_________ c. Who was to receive commandments and revelations for the Church?

_________ d. Why has the Lord given this method to the Church?

_________ e. What were the elders commanded to do during their meetings? Why?

_________ f. What were the elders instructed to do if they desired the glories of the kingdom?

_________ g. What were the elders sent forth to do?

_________ h. Why were the elders to sanctify themselves? (See also v. 16c.)

_________ i. List twelve ways the Lord has called upon the nations of the earth.

_________ j. When will we know the fate of the wicked?

_________ k. What should we allow to "rest upon [our] minds"?

Doctrine and Covenants 44

VERSE NUMBER

_________ a. Where and when was the revelation received that was recorded in Doctrine and Covenants 44?

_________ b. What was required for the Lord to pour out his Spirit at the conference?

_________ c. Why were the Church members to be organized?

________ d. How are the poor and the needy to be treated?

Doctrine and Covenants 45

VERSE NUMBER

________ a. What prevented people from investigating the Church?

________ b. What does the Lord say to the Father in our behalf?

________ c. List four reasons why the Lord has sent his everlasting covenant into the world.

________ d. What happened to the City of Enoch? (See D&C 45:12*a*.)

________ e. What did the disciples of old consider to be a bondage?

________ f. List eleven signs that the times of the Gentiles are to be fulfilled.

________ g. Why will the Gentiles "turn their hearts from [the Lord]"?

________ h. What will those who fear the Lord be looking for?

________ i. List four things they will see.

________ j. List eight things that will happen when the arm of the Lord falls upon the nations. (See vv. 48–50.)

________ k. What will the Lord say to the Jews when they ask about his wounds? (See also vv. 51*b*, 52*a*.)

________ l. What will the Jews then do? Why?

________ m. What will happen to those who knew no law when the Lord comes?

________ n. What will happen to Satan when the Lord comes?

________ o. What is the oil that is referred to in the parable of the ten virgins? (See also v. 56*b*; Matthew 25:1–13; D&C 33:17.)

________ p. What will happen to those who are wise and "have taken the Holy Spirit for their guide"?

________ q. What is the place of their inheritance to be called?

________ r. Who will need to flee to Zion in the last days?

________ s. Why will the wicked "not go up to battle against Zion"?

What effect do verses 3 through 5 have on your desire to learn and keep the commandments?

Doctrine and Covenants 46

VERSE NUMBER

________ a. What was the purpose of the revelation recorded in Doctrine and Covenants 46?

________ b. Who may attend the public meetings of the Church?

_______ c. When should a Church member not partake of the sacrament?

_______ d. What has the Lord commanded Church members to do? Why?

_______ e. Why should we seek earnestly for the best gifts?

_______ f. Why does the Lord give his gifts?

_______ g. List thirteen gifts the Lord mentioned in verses 13 through 25.

_______ h. Why has the Lord appointed someone to discern these gifts?

_______ i. What must we continually practice?

Doctrine and Covenants 47

VERSE NUMBER

_______ a. What had John Whitmer previously done for Joseph Smith?

_______ b. What was John called to do?

_______ c. What would John be given, if he remained faithful, to help him in his calling?

Doctrine and Covenants 48

VERSE NUMBER

_______ a. Why did the Prophet inquire of the Lord?

_______ b. Why was Joseph Smith to save all the money he could?

_________ c. What would certain men be appointed later to do?

Doctrine and Covenants 49

VERSE NUMBER

_________ a. How was the revelation recorded in Doctrine and Covenants 49 received by the Shaker community?

_________ b. What were Sidney Rigdon and Parley P. Pratt to do?

_________ c. What was Leman Copley to do?

_________ d. What was the message of the apostle Peter?

_________ e. For what use has the Lord ordained the beasts and fowls?

_________ f. Why does the world lie in sin?

_________ g. What has the Lord said of those who "wasteth flesh and have no need"?

_________ h. What will happen to the Lamanites before the Lord comes?

Doctrine and Covenants 50

VERSE NUMBER

_________ a. Why was the revelation recorded in Doctrine and Covenants 50 given?

_________ b. What did some Church members claim to be receiving?

_________ c. How had Satan sought to deceive the members of the Church? Why?

_________ d. What is required of us if we are to inherit eternal life?

_________ e. What should we beware of?

_________ f. To what were the elders of the Church ordained?

_________ g. What did the elders do that was not appropriate to their calling?

_________ h. How were the elders to preach the word of God?

________ i. How are we to receive the word of God?

________ j. What happens when the word is preached and received by the Spirit of truth?

________ k. What happens to us as we receive light from God?

________ l. Who is possessor of all things? Why?

________ m. How are the elders to have evil spirits depart? Why?

________ n. Why did the Lord not condemn the brethren?

Why should you live worthy to have the Holy Ghost as your companion? (See also vv. 17–25.)

Doctrine and Covenants 51

VERSE NUMBER

________ a. Why was the revelation recorded in Doctrine and Covenants 51 given?

________ b. In verse 3, what was Edward Partridge instructed to do?

________ c. Under the law of consecration, what was to happen to the property of a person who was excommunicated?

________ d. What was to happen with surplus money?

________ e. How were the Saints to deal with each other?

________ f. What is the purpose of the bishops' storehouse? (See D&C 83:6.)

________ g. What privilege did the Lord grant to his Saints? (See also D&C 51:2.)

________ h. Who shall inherit eternal life?

Doctrine and Covenants 52

VERSE NUMBER

________ a. To whom and when was the revelation recorded in Doctrine and Covenants 52 given?

_______ b. What were Joseph Smith and Sidney Rigdon to do?

_______ c. In verses 9 through 10, what instruction was given to the missionaries?

_______ d. What will happen to "[him] that is faithful"?

_______ e. What is Satan doing? (See also Bible Dictionary, p. 657, s.v. "Devil.")

_______ f. How can we discern that which is of God? (See also Moroni 7:12–19.)

_______ g. In verses 22 through 32 of Doctrine and Covenants 52, where were the missionaries called to serve?

_______ h. What blessing would these missionaries receive if they were faithful?

_______ i. Why were the other elders to labor with their own hands?

_______ j. What is required of a disciple of the Lord?

Doctrine and Covenants 53

VERSE NUMBER

_______ a. Why was the revelation recorded in Doctrine and Covenants 53 given?

_______ b. What had Sidney Gilbert prayed for?

_______ c. What was Sidney commanded to do?

_______ d. What did the Lord want Sidney to learn?

Doctrine and Covenants 54

VERSE NUMBER

_______ a. Why was the revelation recorded in Doctrine and Covenants 54 given?

_______ b. How were the brethren to escape their enemies?

_______ c. How did the Lord view the covenant they had made?

_______ d. Why were they instructed to "flee the land"?

_________ e. Where were they to go?

Doctrine and Covenants 55

VERSE NUMBER

_________ a. Why was the revelation recorded in Doctrine and Covenants 55 given?

_________ b. What would happen to William Phelps after his baptism?

_________ c. List three things that Joseph Smith was to ordain William to do.

_________ d. Where was William to do this work? (See also D&C 52:42.)

Doctrine and Covenants 56

VERSE NUMBER

_________ a. Why was the revelation recorded in Doctrine and Covenants 56 given?

_________ b. What will be the fate of those who do not obey the Lord's commands?

_________ c. What was Newell Knight to do?

_________ d. What was Ezra Thayre to do?

_________ e. Why were the sins of the Saints not pardoned?

_________ f. Why are many of the rich under condemnation?

_________ g. Why are many of the poor under condemnation?

_________ h. Who of the poor will be blessed? How?

Doctrine and Covenants 57

VERSE NUMBER

_________ a. Where and when was the revelation recorded in Doctrine and Covenants 57 given?

_________ b. Where had the elders traveled?

_________ c. What had the Prophet Joseph Smith prayed to know?

_________ d. Where is the center place for the gathering of the Saints? (See also Map, p. 297.)

_________ e. What was Sidney Gilbert to do?

_________ f. What was Edward Partridge to do?

_________ g. What was William W. Phelps to do?

_________ h. What was Oliver Cowdery to do?

_________ i. What were the bishop and his agent to do?

Doctrine and Covenants 58

VERSE NUMBER

_________ a. What were many Church members eager to know?

_________ b. What were the Saints not able to understand?

_________ c. What will come before the blessings? Why?

_________ d. List six reasons why the Lord brought the elders to Zion. (See D&C 58:6–13.)

_________ e. What were the sins of Edward Partridge?

_________ f. What was Edward appointed to do?

_________ g. Why is "no man [to] break the laws of the land"?

_________ h. Why should we not have to be commanded "in all things"?

________ i. What should we be continually doing?

________ j. What power do we have to earn our reward?

________ k. Whose "reward lurketh beneath and not from above"?

________ l. What will the Lord do for us when we repent of our sins?

________ m. What is required of us to repent? (See also Bible Dictionary, p. 649, s.v. "Confession.")

________ n. Why was Ziba Peterson released from his calling?

________ o. What was to "go forth from this place"?

What is your attitude toward your responsibilities at Church and at home? (See D&C 58:26–28.)

Doctrine and Covenants 59

VERSE NUMBER

________ a. Where and when was the revelation recorded in Doctrine and Covenants 59 received?

________ b. What was done in the land of Zion?

________ c. To whom were these commandments especially applicable?

________ d. Who did the Lord say were blessed?

________ e. What commandments were given that compare with those given in Matthew 22:36–40?

________ f. What other commandments were given?

________ g. What are we to do on the Sabbath day? (See also Bible Dictionary, p. 764, s.v. "Sabbath.")

________ h. What blessings do we receive for keeping the Sabbath day holy?

________ i. Against whom is the wrath of God kindled?

Doctrine and Covenants 60

VERSE NUMBER

________ a. What did the elders desire to know?

________ b. Why was the Lord not pleased with some elders?

________ c. What would happen if the elders were not more faithful?

________ d. How were the elders to get to St. Louis?

________ e. What commandment was given to the rest of the elders?

________ f. Why were they to "shake off the dust of [their] feet" against those who did not receive them and also to "wash [their] feet"? (See also D&C 60:15*a*; 75:20; 84:92.)

Doctrine and Covenants 61

VERSE NUMBER

________ a. What had William W. Phelps seen in his vision?

________ b. To whom is the Lord merciful?

________ c. Why should the elders not have been "moving swiftly upon the waters"?

________ d. Where will no flesh be safe in the last days?

________ e. Why has the Lord blessed the land?

________ f. How were the Saints to travel to Zion?

________ g. What counsel did the Lord give the elders in Doctrine and Covenants 61:36–39?

Doctrine and Covenants 62

VERSE NUMBER

________ a. Who did the Prophet Joseph Smith and his group meet while traveling to Kirtland?

________ b. How were those blessed who were traveling to Zion?

________ c. What were they to do?

________ d. Why had the Lord brought these two groups together?

Doctrine and Covenants 63

VERSE NUMBER

________ a. What was the "most important temporal object in view"?

________ b. Why was the revelation recorded in Doctrine and Covenants 63 given?

________ c. Upon whom will the day of wrath come?

________ d. What is not obtained by signs?

________ e. What is required for signs to be given?

________ f. What is required to please God?

________ g. What kind of thoughts will deprive us of the Spirit?

________ h. Who will not have part in the first resurrection?

________ i. To whom will the Lord give the mysteries of his kingdom?

________ j. Why were the Saints not to gather to Zion in haste?

________ k. What had Satan put into the hearts of some people?

________ l. Who shall slay the wicked?

________ m. Who would decide who was to go to Zion and who was to stay?

________ n. How long will the body and the spirit be separated for those who die after the Lord comes?

________ o. What was Sidney Rigdon to do? Why?

________ p. What should we remember about "that which cometh from above"?

Doctrine and Covenants 64

VERSE NUMBER

________ a. What was happening at the time the revelation recorded in Doctrine and Covenants 64 was received?

________ b. Whose sins does the Lord forgive?

________ c. Why were the disciples of old "afflicted and sorely chastened"?

________ d. In whom does the greater sin remain when a trespass occurs?

________ e. Who does the Lord require you to forgive?

________ f. What should we say in our heart when we are offended?

________ g. Why should we bring those who do not repent before the elders of the Church?

________ h. How long were some members required to stay in Kirtland, Ohio?

________ i. Who will not be burned at the coming of the Lord?

________ j. Why are we to "be not weary in well-doing"?

________ k. Upon whom will the glory of the Lord rest?

Doctrine and Covenants 65

VERSE NUMBER

________ a. How did the Prophet Joseph Smith designate this revelation?

________ b. What is committed to man on the earth?

________ c. What will happen to the gospel?

________ d. What is required of the Saints?

_____ e. What is the difference between the kingdom of God and the kingdom of heaven? (See also Bible Dictionary, p. 721, s.v. "kingdom of heaven.")

Doctrine and Covenants 66

VERSE NUMBER

_____ a. Why was the revelation given that is recorded in Doctrine and Covenants 66?

_____ b. Why was William E. McLellin blessed?

_____ c. How was he to know what to repent of?

_____ d. List eleven things William was instructed to do.

_____ e. What blessing was promised William if he was faithful?

Doctrine and Covenants 67

VERSE NUMBER

_____ a. Why was the revelation recorded in Doctrine and Covenants 67 given?

_____ b. How many of the brethren knew the revelations were true?

_____ c. Why did the elders fail to receive the blessing the Lord offered to them?

_____ d. How could the elders have been justified in saying they didn't know if the revelations were true?

_____ e. How would the elders be under condemnation?

_____ f. What promise did the Lord make to the elders?

________ g. Why were they not able to see God at that time?

Doctrine and Covenants 68

VERSE NUMBER

________ a. Why was the revelation recorded in Doctrine and Covenants 68 given?

________ b. How is scripture received?

________ c. How does the Lord define scripture?

________ d. What was the word of the Lord to the faithful elders of the Church?

________ e. How is a priesthood bearer called to be a bishop?

________ f. Who has a legal right to the office of bishop?

________ g. What are the parents in Zion to teach their children?

________ h. What are children in Zion to do when they are eight years old?

________ i. List four reasons why the Lord was not pleased with "the inhabitants of Zion"?

Doctrine and Covenants 69

VERSE NUMBER

________ a. What was Oliver Cowdery appointed to do at the conference?

________ b. Why was John Whitmer to travel with Oliver?

________ c. What else was John called to do?

________ d. What were the missionaries to do?

________ e. How was John to obtain the knowledge required for his history?

Doctrine and Covenants 70

VERSE NUMBER

________ a. What was the original name of the Doctrine and Covenants?

_________ b. Unto what were the brethren named in Doctrine and Covenants 70:1 appointed and ordained?

_________ c. What will the Lord require of them in the Day of Judgment?

_________ d. How were the profits from the sale of the Book of Commandments to be used? (See also v. 8*a*; 72:20–22.)

_________ e. How are those who administer in spiritual things to receive more than those administering in temporal things?

_________ f. How would the Saints be blessed by being equal in their temporal things?

Doctrine and Covenants 71

VERSE NUMBER

_________ a. What was the Prophet doing when this revelation was received?

_________ b. How were Joseph Smith and Sidney Rigdon to proclaim the gospel?

_________ c. For what were they to "prepare the way"?

_________ d. Why is it important that we use our gifts and talents?

_________ e. How were Joseph and Sidney to soften the hearts of those who had unfriendly feelings toward the Church?

_________ f. How would the Lord protect them?

Doctrine and Covenants 72

VERSE NUMBER

_________ a. Why had several elders and members met in Kirtland?

_________ b. What does the Lord require of every steward?

_________ c. What is the inheritance of the faithful and wise?

_________ d. Who did the Lord choose to be the bishop in Kirtland?

_________ e. What was the bishop to do? (See D&C 72:10–11.)

________ f. Why was the bishop to issue a certificate to each elder going to Zion?

________ g. List three reasons why those elders responsible to publish the revelations were entitled to assistance.

________ h. What must be done by every member of the Church who comes to Zion?

Doctrine and Covenants 73

VERSE NUMBER

________ a. What had Joseph Smith and Sidney Rigdon been doing in the past month?

________ b. Who was to continue to preach? (See D&C 73:1*a*.)

________ c. What were Joseph and Sidney to do?

Doctrine and Covenants 74

VERSE NUMBER

________ a. What was Joseph Smith doing when he received the revelation recorded in Doctrine and Covenants 74?

________ b. Why was there "a great contention among the people" in the days of the apostles of old?

________ c. Why had the apostle Paul given the commandment recorded in 1 Corinthians 7:14?

Doctrine and Covenants 75

VERSE NUMBER

________ a. Why did certain elders desire to know more about their duties?

________ b. What were the elders instructed to do?

________ c. How were the faithful missionaries to be rewarded?

________ d. Who were to go to the south countries?

_________ e. What was Luke Johnson to do during his mission?

_________ f. Who were to go to the eastern countries?

_________ g. Who were to go to the western countries?

_________ h. What were the missionaries to leave upon the house of them who received them?

_________ i. What was the duty of the Church toward the families of the missionaries?

_________ j. Who "shall not have place in the Church"?

Doctrine and Covenants 76

VERSE NUMBER

_________ a. To whom was the vision given that is recorded in Doctrine and Covenants 76?

_________ b. What had been taken or lost from the Bible when it was compiled?

_________ c. List nine blessings that those who fear and serve the Lord in truth will receive? (See also Bible Dictionary, p. 672, s.v. "fear.")

_________ d. What happened to Joseph Smith and Sidney Rigdon by the power of the Spirit?

_________ e. With whom did they speak?

_________ f. List six things they included in their testimony.

_________ g. Who are the sons of perdition?

_________ h. What is the fate of the sons of perdition?

_________ i. List twelve characteristics of those who shall "come forth in the resurrection of the just." (See D&C 51–60; see also Bible Dictionary, p. 655, s.v. "Degrees of Glory.")

_________ j. List nine things Joseph and Sidney recorded about the final glory of the just. (See D&C 76:62–70.)

_________ k. List five things they recorded about those in the terrestrial world. (See vv. 71–75, 79.)

_________ l. Who will visit the terrestrial world?

________ m. List thirteen things they recorded about those in the telestial world. (See vv. 82–85, 101–10.)

________ n. Who will visit the telestial world?

________ o. Where does God the Father reign upon his throne?

________ p. Who does the Father make "equal in power, and in might, and in dominion"?

________ q. To whom does God grant the "privilege of seeing and knowing for themselves"?

List three things that you can begin doing to obtain a celestial body.

Doctrine and Covenants 77

VERSE NUMBER

________ a. What was the Prophet Joseph doing at the time he received the revelation recorded in Doctrine and Covenants 77? (See also Bible Dictionary, p. 762, s.v. "Revelation of John.")

________ b. In Revelation 4, what did John see? (See Revelation 4 headnote.)

________ c. What is the earth to be like in its sanctified, eternal state?

________ d. Who, besides people, have spirits?

________ e. What is represented by the eyes and wings of the beast?

________ f. How many years of temporal existence (from the fall of Adam to the end of the Millennium) will the earth have?

________ g. What is represented by each seal?

________ h. What did John see in the sixth seal? (See Revelation 7 headnote.)

________ i. In Revelation 7:1, what power do the four angels have?

________ j. Who is the angel "ascending from the east"?

________ k. When are the things recorded in Revelation chapter 7 to be accomplished? (See also Revelation 7 headnote.)

________ l. What are the 144,000 ordained to do?

________ m. In Revelation 8 and 9, what did John see? (See headnotes to Revelation 8–9.)

________ n. When will the angels sound their seven trumpets? Why?

________ o. When will the things recorded in Revelation 9 be accomplished?

________ p. What is John to do in the last days? (See Revelation 10 headnote.)

________ q. What will happen to the two witnesses (prophets) in Jerusalem? (See Revelation 11 headnote.)

Doctrine and Covenants 78

VERSE NUMBER

________ a. What is the purpose of the revelation recorded in Doctrine and Covenants 78?

________ b. What had the time come for in the Church?

________ c. What is required before we can become equal in heavenly things?

_________ d. What is required if we are to live in the celestial world?

_________ e. What does Satan seek to do?

_________ f. What were the brethren commanded to do? Why?

_________ g. Who is Michael? (See v. 16*a*.)

_________ h. Why is it important for us to thank the Lord in all things?

Doctrine and Covenants 79

VERSE NUMBER

_________ a. To whom was the revelation recorded in Doctrine and Covenants 79 given?

_________ b. What did the Lord instruct him to do?

_________ c. What would the Comforter do for Jared Carter?

_________ d. What blessing would Jared receive if he was faithful?

Doctrine and Covenants 80

VERSE NUMBER

_________ a. To whom was given the revelation recorded in Doctrine and Covenants 80?

_________ b. What did the Lord instruct him to do?

_________ c. What was Stephen Burnett to declare?

Doctrine and Covenants 81

VERSE NUMBER

_________ a. What office was called for by this revelation?

_________ b. What was Frederick G. Williams called to be?

_________ c. To whom do the keys of the kingdom belong?

________ d. List five things Frederick was instructed to do.

________ e. How would he be rewarded if he was faithful?

Doctrine and Covenants 82

VERSE NUMBER

________ a. Where and when was the revelation recorded in Doctrine and Covenants 82 received?

________ b. How do we obtain forgiveness for our trespasses?

________ c. What will bring "sore judgments" upon the heads of the members?

________ d. Who will receive the greater condemnation?

________ e. How is it possible to ensure the Lord will fulfill his promises?

________ f. Why were the brethren to be bound together by covenant?

________ g. Whose interest were they to seek?

________ h. What will happen to the soul of someone who hardens his heart?

________ i. Why did the Lord encourage the Saints to make friends with their neighbors?

Doctrine and Covenants 83

VERSE NUMBER

________ a. What was Joseph Smith doing when the revelation recorded in Doctrine and Covenants 83 was received?

________ b. Who do women with husbands have claim on for their support?

________ c. Who do faithful women whose husbands have been taken have claim on for their support?

________ d. Who do children have claim on for their support?

________ e. Who is the storehouse to provide for?

Doctrine and Covenants 84

VERSE NUMBER

________ a. Why were the elders in Kirtland?

________ b. What were Joseph Smith and six elders doing when this revelation was given?

________ c. What city will be built in the western part of Missouri?

________ d. What will be built in "this generation"?

________ e. Trace the lineage of the priesthood from Adam to Moses.

________ f. What does the Melchizedek Priesthood do?

________ g. What is required of us if we are to see the face of God the Father and live?

________ h. Why did Moses seek diligently to sanctify his people?

________ i. What is the preparatory gospel that is administered by the Aaronic Priesthood?

________ j. What was John the Baptist ordained by an angel to do when he was only eight days old?

________ k. Who are sanctified by the Spirit "unto the renewing of their bodies"?

________ l. What are the terms of the oath and covenant of the priesthood?

________ m. How are we to live?

________ n. What is the relationship between the word of the Lord, truth, light, and spirit? (See also Bible Dictionary, p. 725, s.v."Light of Christ.")

________ o. How do we come unto the Father? (See also Moroni 7:13–17.)

________ p. How do we know if people are under the bondage of sin?

________ q. Why have their minds been darkened in the past?

________ r. What is required if we are not to come under the Lord's condemnation?

________ s. List seven signs that follow those who believe.

________ t. What is required of those who know of these signs? Why?

________ u. How does the Lord refer to these elders?

________ v. What promises did the Lord make to the faithful missionaries?

________ w. When will the plagues be taken from the earth?

________ x. Why should the strong in spirit take the weak with them?

________ y. What should every member of the Church do? Why?

Doctrine and Covenants 85

VERSE NUMBER

________ a. To whom was the revelation recorded in Doctrine and Covenants 85 sent? Why?

________ b. What is the duty of the Lord's clerk?

________ c. Whose names are not to be on the records of the Church?

________ d. Who will not find an inheritance among the Saints of God?

Doctrine and Covenants 86

VERSE NUMBER

________ a. What was the Prophet Joseph doing at the time the revelation recorded in Doctrine and Covenants 86 was received?

________ b. What is the parable of the wheat and the tares? (See Matthew 13:13–43.)

________ c. What is the field?

________ d. Who are the sowers of the seed?

________ e. Who is the sower of the tares?

________ f. Why was the Lord making the angels wait to destroy the tares?

________ g. Who will be gathered first?

Doctrine and Covenants 87

VERSE NUMBER

________ a. What thoughts were on the minds of the brethren when the revelation recorded in Doctrine and Covenants 87 was received?

________ b. Where would the Civil War begin?

________ c. Who would the slaves rise up against?

________ d. Who will trouble and distress the Gentiles? (See D&C 109:65; see also 87:5*a*.)

________ e. How will the people of the earth feel the chastening of the Lord?

________ f. Where are the Saints to stand until the Lord comes?

Doctrine and Covenants 88

VERSE NUMBER

________ a. What is the message of the Lord in the revelation recorded in Doctrine and Covenants 88?

________ b. To whom was this revelation directed?

________ c. Where were their prayers recorded?

________ d. Who is the Second Comforter? (See Bible Dictionary, p. 648, s.v. "Comforter.")

_________ e. What is the Second Comforter a promise of?

_________ f. What is the soul of man?

_________ g. What is required for the earth to be prepared for its celestial glory? (See also D&C 88:19*a*.)

_________ h. Why was the earth created?

_________ i. What must we abide in order to abide the celestial glory?

_________ j. What type of body and glory will a celestial spirit receive?

_________ k. Who are those that will remain filthy?

_________ l. Who will the faithful comprehend? How?

_________ m. In verse 62, what commandment did the Lord give?

_________ n. Why do we need to be careful about what we ask for in our prayers?

_________ o. Why is it necessary for us to sanctify ourselves?

_________ p. In verse 69, what are we instructed to do?

_________ q. What commandment did the Lord give in verse 74? In verse 76? In verse 77?

_________ r. Why should we "teach diligently"?

_________ s. What is the responsibility of those who have been warned? Why?

_________ t. What will happen in the near future? (See also D&C 29:14.)

_________ u. What will happen when each of the seven angels sounds his trump?

_________ v. What will happen when the face of the Lord is unveiled?

_________ w. What will happen at the "battle of the great God"?

_________ x. In Doctrine and Covenants 88:118–26, what instructions were given to the Saints?

_________ y. What was the purpose of the "school of the prophets"?

Doctrine and Covenants 89

VERSE NUMBER

_________ a. Why was the revelation recorded in Doctrine and Covenants 89 given?

_________ b. What is this revelation known as?

_________ c. How was this revelation originally to have been received?

_________ d. Why has the Lord given us the Word of Wisdom?

_________ e. What are strong drinks (alcohol) to be used for?

_________ f. What is tobacco to be used for?

_________ g. How are herbs and fruits to be used?

_________ h. How is the flesh of animals to be used?

_________ i. List four blessings the Lord has promised those who are faithful in obeying the Word of Wisdom and the other commandments.

Why should you obey the Word of Wisdom?

Doctrine and Covenants 90

VERSE NUMBER

_________ a. What quorum in the Church does the revelation recorded in Doctrine and Covenants 90 concern?

_________ b. Why do those who receive the revelations of God need to beware?

_________ c. How were Sidney Rigdon and Frederick G. Williams equal with Joseph Smith?

________ d. For what purpose will the arm of the Lord be revealed in power?

________ e. How will "every man . . . hear the fulness of the gospel"?

________ f. What was Joseph to do when he finished his translation of the Bible?

________ g. What was Vienna Jacques instructed to do?

________ h. Why do the angels rejoice over the brethren in Zion?

________ i. What will the Lord do to ensure that Zion becomes clean?

Doctrine and Covenants 91

VERSE NUMBER

________ a. What was Joseph Smith doing when he received the revelation recorded in Doctrine and Covenants 91?

________ b. What did the Lord say about the Apocrypha? (See also Bible Dictionary, p. 610, s.v. "Apocrypha.")

________ c. How is the Apocrypha to be understood?

Doctrine and Covenants 92

VERSE NUMBER

________ a. To whom was given the revelation recorded in Doctrine and Covenants 92?

________ b. Into what was Frederick G. Williams to be received?

________ c. What kind of member in the united order was he to be?

Doctrine and Covenants 93

VERSE NUMBER

________ a. Where and when was the revelation recorded in Doctrine and Covenants 93 received?

________ b. Who will see the face of the Lord and know that he lives?

________ c. What has yet to be revealed concerning John's record?

________ d. Why was Jesus called the Son of God?

________ e. In what form did the Holy Ghost descend upon Jesus?

________ f. Why has the Lord given these sayings to us?

________ g. Who was in the beginning with the Father?

________ h. What is truth?

________ i. What is the only way to receive a fulness of truth?

________ j. What is required for us to know all things?

________ k. Who are under condemnation?

________ l. What is the glory of God?

________ m. What does the glory of God do?

________ n. How does Satan take away light and truth?

________ o. How are children to be brought up?

________ p. Why are we to pray always?

________ q. What were the brethren to do after the Bible was translated?

Doctrine and Covenants 94

VERSE NUMBER

________ a. What committee was formed by the revelation recorded in Doctrine and Covenants 94?

________ b. What were the brethren to begin doing?

________ c. What was the purpose of the house for the presidency?

________ d. What would happen if "any unclean thing" entered this house?

_________ e. What was the second lot to be used for?

Doctrine and Covenants 95

VERSE NUMBER

_________ a. Where and when was the revelation recorded in Doctrine and Covenants 95 received?

_________ b. Why does the Lord chasten those he loves?

_________ c. What "very grievous sin" had the brethren committed?

_________ d. What was the sin of those who were called but not chosen?

_________ e. Why did the Lord command them to build a temple?

_________ f. Why did the Lord send forth his servants "to be chastened"?

_________ g. Why did the Saints need to keep the commandments to build the temple?

_________ h. To what purpose was the lower part of the temple to be dedicated?

_________ i. To what purpose was the upper part of the temple to be dedicated?

Doctrine and Covenants 96

VERSE NUMBER

_________ a. Why did the Saints "inquire of the Lord"?

_________ b. What was most urgent to the Lord? Why?

_________ c. What promise was given to John Johnson?

_________ d. Why did the Lord want him to be a member of the united order?

Doctrine and Covenants 97

VERSE NUMBER

_________ a. Why had the Prophet inquired of the Lord?

_________ b. What were many of the Saints in Zion seeking diligently to do?

_________ c. How was Parley P. Pratt to be blessed?

_________ d. Which people were accepted of the Lord?

_________ e. How was the temple in the land of Zion to be built?

_________ f. Why was the temple to be built?

_________ g. Who will the pure in heart see?

_________ h. What will happen if Zion does these things?

_________ i. What is Zion? (See Bible Dictionary, p. 792, s.v. "Zion.")

_________ j. How will Zion escape the Lord's scourge?

_________ k. What will happen if Zion does not keep the commandments?

Doctrine and Covenants 98

VERSE NUMBER

_________ a. Why was the revelation recorded in Doctrine and Covenants 98 given?

_________ b. How many miles is Missouri from Kirtland, Ohio?

_________ c. What did the Lord do with the prayers of the Saints?

_________ d. Why are we to support the Constitution of the United States?

_________ e. When do the people mourn?

_________ f. What type of people "should be sought for diligently" to fill government office?

_________ g. What will the Lord give to the faithful?

_________ h. Why were the Saints not to be afraid of their enemies?

_________ i. What would the Lord do to the Saints in Kirtland if they did not repent?

________ j. What will be our reward if we do not retaliate after being smitten by our enemy the first time? The second time? The third time?

________ k. What will stand as a testimony against our enemy in the last day?

________ l. What will the Lord do if our enemy has been warned in his name but comes against us a fourth time?

________ m. To whom was this law previously given?

________ n. Under what conditions were the ancients justified in going to battle?

________ o. How many times are we required to forgive our enemy if he does not repent?

________ p. What is required for our enemy's sins to be blotted out after the fourth offense?

Doctrine and Covenants 99

VERSE NUMBER

________ a. To whom was the revelation recorded in Doctrine and Covenants 99 given?

________ b. What was John Murdock called to do?

________ c. What power was he to have?

________ d. What was he to do before he went on his mission?

Doctrine and Covenants 100

VERSE NUMBER

________ a. Who were Joseph Smith and Sidney Rigdon concerned about? Why?

________ b. What did the Lord say concerning their families?

________ c. Why had the Lord brought them to this place?

________ d. What were they to do?

________ e. What would the Lord do for them?

________ f. What commandment did they receive?

________ g. What blessing was promised for keeping this commandment?

________ h. What was Sidney called to do?

________ i. What power was Joseph to have?

________ j. What power was Sidney to have?

________ k. What will the Lord "raise up unto" himself?

Doctrine and Covenants 101

VERSE NUMBER

________ a. What was happening to the Saints in Missouri?

________ b. Why did the Lord allow the Saints to be driven from their inheritance?

________ c. What is required of us if we are to be sanctified?

________ d. How did the Saints pollute their inheritance?

________ e. Why was the Lord slow to answer their prayers?

________ f. Where were the Saints to gather?

________ g. List nine things that will happen when the Lord comes again.

________ h. Who will "partake of all this glory"?

________ i. Who are "the salt of the earth"?

________ j. Why were the children of Zion chastened by the Lord?

________ k. Who are to be appointed to purchase the lands in Zion?

________ l. Why did the Lord establish the Constitution?

________ m. What verse instructs the Saints not to sell their land in Missouri?

Doctrine and Covenants 102

VERSE NUMBER

________ a. Doctrine and Covenants 102 is the minutes of what meeting?

________ b. What is the purpose of the high council of the Church?

________ c. Who is to nominate replacements when a vacancy occurs in this council?

________ d. How many of the high council are to represent the accused? Why?

________ e. The decision of which council cannot be appealed?

Doctrine and Covenants 103

VERSE NUMBER

________ a. Why had Parley P. Pratt and Lyman Wight come from Missouri?

________ b. List two reasons why the Lord allowed the Saints in Zion to be persecuted?

________ c. How were the Saints to prevail against their enemies?

________ d. What would happen if the Saints did not obey the Lord? Why?

________ e. What blessing did the Lord promise to the faithful after their trials?

________ f. What did the Lord require of Sidney Rigdon?

________ g. How many men were to travel to Zion with Parley and Lyman?

_________ h. How are victory and glory obtained?

Doctrine and Covenants 104

VERSE NUMBER

_________ a. What is the revelation recorded in Doctrine and Covenants 104 about?

_________ b. How had some Saints broken their covenant?

_________ c. How did the Lord chasten them?

_________ d. What is the fate of those who are "cut off for transgression"?

_________ e. What power did the Lord give to the brethren?

_________ f. How has the Lord decreed he would provide for his Saints?

_________ g. What has the Lord "given unto the children of men"?

_________ h. To whom should we give our surplus?

_________ i. Why was the united order dissolved?

_________ j. What was to be delivered "into the treasury"?

_________ k. What was the purpose of the second treasury?

_________ l. What were the brethren to do about their debts?

Doctrine and Covenants 105

VERSE NUMBER

_________ a. What was happening to the Saints in Missouri?

_________ b. What was Zion's Camp taking to them?

_________ c. What had prevented the Saints from being redeemed?

_________ d. How is Zion to be built?

_________ e. Why were the elders to receive their temple endowments?

_________ f. What was the purpose of Zion's Camp?

_________ g. How were the Saints to conduct themselves?

_________ h. Why did the Lord instruct the brethren to purchase as much land as possible in Zion?

_________ i. How will those who are chosen obtain the power to establish Zion?

_________ j. What were the Saints instructed to do with those who had "smitten" them?

Doctrine and Covenants 106

VERSE NUMBER

_________ a. To whom was the revelation recorded in Doctrine and Covenants 106 directed?

_________ b. To what office was Warren Cowdery to be ordained?

_________ c. What did the Lord instruct him to do?

_________ d. What was the response in heaven when Warren repented of his sins?

What do you think the response in heaven is when you repent?

Doctrine and Covenants 107

VERSE NUMBER

_________ a. Where were the Twelve preparing to go?

_________ b. Why is the first priesthood named after Melchizedek? (See also Bible Dictionary, p. 730, s.v. "Melchizedek.")

_________ c. What power and authority does the Melchizedek Priesthood hold? (See also Bible Dictionary, p. 730, s.v. "Melchizedek Priesthood.")

_________ d. Who has the right to officiate when a high priest is not present?

_________ e. What things are "the high priest and elder" to administer in?

_________ f. What power does the Aaronic Priesthood have?

_________ g. Who forms the quorum of the Presidency of the Church?

_________ h. What are the Twelve Apostles called to do?

_________ i. What are the Seventies called to do?

_________ j. What is required when a decision is to be made by one of the quorums?

_________ k. What promise is given to those who do these things?

_________ l. What promise was given to Seth? Why?

_________ m. Who ordained Enoch?

_________ n. What did Adam do three years before he died?

_________ o. What is the duty of a bishop who is not a literal descendant of Aaron?

_________ p. What is the highest council of the Church?

_________ q. What is "the duty of a president over the office of a deacon"?

_________ r. What is the duty of the President of the Church?

_________ s. What is required of every member of the Church?

Doctrine and Covenants 108

VERSE NUMBER

_________ a. Why did Lyman Sherman receive the revelation now recorded in Doctrine and Covenants 108?

_________ b. Why was Lyman able to let his "soul be at rest concerning [his] spiritual standing"?

_________ c. What was he to wait patiently for?

________ d. How was Lyman to strengthen his brethren?

Doctrine and Covenants 109

VERSE NUMBER

________ a. What is the revelation recorded in Doctrine and Covenants 109? (See also Bible Dictionary, p. 780, s.v. "Temple.")

________ b. In verse 4 of Doctrine and Covenants 109, what was asked of the Father?

________ c. What did the people sacrifice to build this temple?

________ d. What should have been felt by all people who entered this temple?

________ e. Why were those who entered this house to be taught wisdom and to seek learning?

________ f. What was this house to be?

________ g. What was not allowed in the temple?

________ h. Why were the servants of God to "go forth from this house armed with [God's] power"?

________ i. What protection for the Saints was the Lord asked to provide?

________ j. What must the hearts of the Saints be prepared for?

________ k. What cities was the Lord asked to bless with peace? Why?

________ l. What was the Lord asked to do with the wicked mob in Missouri?

________ m. What was requested concerning the "scattered remnants of Israel"?

________ n. What was requested concerning Joseph Smith and his family?

________ o. What was requested in verse 78?

Doctrine and Covenants 110

VERSE NUMBER

________ a. Where was the vision recorded in Doctrine and Covenants 110 received?

________ b. Who saw this vision?

________ c. How did they describe the Lord?

________ d. Why were they to "lift up [their] heads and rejoice"?

________ e. Why were those who built the temple "with their might" to rejoice?

________ f. Upon what conditions would the Lord appear and speak to his servants?

________ g. Why did Moses appear to them? (See also Bible Dictionary, p. 84, s.v. "Dispensation.")

________ h. Why did Elias appear to them?

________ i. Why did Elijah appear to them?

Doctrine and Covenants 111

VERSE NUMBER

________ a. Why were the Church leaders in debt?

________ b. Why did the Church leaders go to Salem?

________ c. What were they instructed to do as they "shall be led"?

________ d. Why were they not to be concerned about their debts?

________ e. How were the brethren to know where to stay?

Doctrine and Covenants 112

VERSE NUMBER

________ a. What position did Thomas B. Marsh hold?

________ b. What was required for Thomas to be exalted?

________ c. From Doctrine and Covenants 112:4–12, list six things Thomas was to do.

_________ d. Why should we be humble?

_________ e. Who had Thomas prayed for?

_________ f. What were the Twelve instructed to do?

_________ g. What "cometh speedily upon the inhabitants of the earth"? Why?

_________ h. Where will the vengeance of the Lord begin?

_________ i. Why were the Twelve required to cleanse their hearts and their garments?

_________ j. How will each of us be rewarded?

Doctrine and Covenants 113

VERSE NUMBER

_________ a. Whose writings were clarified by the revelation recorded in Doctrine and Covenants 113?

_________ b. Who is the stem of Jesse?

_________ c. What is the rod?

_________ d. What is the root?

_________ e. What is meant by the phrase "Put on thy strength, O Zion"?

_________ f. What are the bands upon the neck of Zion?

Doctrine and Covenants 114

VERSE NUMBER

_________ a. Where and when was the revelation recorded in Doctrine and Covenants 114 received?

_________ b. What was David W. Patten to do?

_________ c. What happens to positions held by those who leave the Church?

Doctrine and Covenants 115

VERSE NUMBER

_________ a. Where and when was the revelation recorded in Doctrine and Covenants 115 received?

_________ b. To whom was this revelation addressed?

_________ c. What was to be the name of the Lord's church?

_________ d. Why are the Saints to gather to Zion and her stakes?

_________ e. What will the city of Far West be? Why?

_________ f. Why were the Saints to build a house unto the Lord?

_________ g. What was the will of the Lord concerning Far West?

Doctrine and Covenants 116

VERSE NUMBER

_________ a. Where and when was the revelation recorded in Doctrine and Covenants 116 received?

_________ b. What name had the Lord given this place? Why? (See Bible Dictionary, p. 604, s.v. "Adam.")

Doctrine and Covenants 117

VERSE NUMBER

_________ a. Where and when was the revelation recorded in Doctrine and Covenants 117 received?

_________ b. What were William Marks and Newel K. Whitney to do?

_________ c. Why were they not to be concerned about their property in Kirtland?

_________ d. Where did Adam live after leaving the Garden of Eden?

________ e. What was Newel to do?

________ f. What was Oliver Granger to do for the benefit of the people?

Doctrine and Covenants 118

VERSE NUMBER

________ a. Why was the revelation recorded in Doctrine and Covenants 118 given?

________ b. Why was Thomas B. Marsh to remain in the land of Zion?

________ c. Upon what conditions would the Lord provide for the families of the Twelve?

________ d. Where were the Twelve to go the next spring? Why?

________ e. Who were appointed to replace the apostles who had been excommunicated?

Doctrine and Covenants 119

VERSE NUMBER

________ a. What law was given in the revelation recorded in Doctrine and Covenants 119?

________ b. What law had previously been revoked? Why?

________ c. How much are the Saints to pay as a tithe? (See Bible Dictionary, p. 785, s.v. "Tithe.")

________ d. How is the land of Zion sanctified?

Doctrine and Covenants 120

VERSE NUMBER

________ a. When and where was the revelation recorded in Doctrine and Covenants 120 received?

________ b. Under whose direction are the tithing funds of the Church to be spent?

Doctrine and Covenants 121

VERSE NUMBER

________ a. Where was Doctrine and Covenants 121 written?

_________ b. What had failed to bring relief to Joseph Smith and his brethren?

_________ c. What questions did Joseph ask of the Lord?

_________ d. What did Joseph ask the Lord to do?

_________ e. What comfort was given to Joseph?

_________ f. Why do enemies "cry transgression"?

_________ g. For whom has the Lord prepared a "swift judgment"?

_________ h. How will God reveal his knowledge?

_________ i. Why are "many called, but few are chosen"?

_________ j. What is the only way the powers of heaven can be controlled or handled?

_________ k. Why is the authority of the priesthood taken from men?

_________ l. What happens to most people as soon as they get a little authority?

_________ m. How is power or influence to be maintained? Why?

_________ n. What is required of us after we reprove someone "with sharpness"? Why?

_________ o. What must we do for our "confidence [to] wax strong in the presence of God" and for the Holy Ghost to be our "constant companion"?

Doctrine and Covenants 122

VERSE NUMBER

_________ a. Where was the revelation recorded in Doctrine and Covenants 122 received?

_________ b. Who will seek "counsel, and authority, and blessings constantly" from Joseph Smith?

_________ c. What was the purpose of the trials mentioned in verses 5 through 7?

_________ d. Why was Joseph not to fear what man can do?

Doctrine and Covenants 123

VERSE NUMBER

_________ a. Where was the revelation recorded in Doctrine and Covenants 123 received?

_________ b. What were the Saints to do in response to persecution?

_________ c. Why were the Saints to seek redress for their persecutions?

_________ d. What was enough to "make hell itself shudder, . . . and the hands of the very devil to tremble"?

_________ e. Why are many kept from the truth?

_________ f. What was required of the Saints before the Lord's arm would be revealed?

Doctrine and Covenants 124

VERSE NUMBER

_________ a. Where and when was the revelation recorded in Doctrine and Covenants 124 received?

_________ b. Why were the Saints compelled to leave Missouri?

_________ c. What was Joseph Smith instructed to make immediately?

_________ d. To whom was this proclamation to be made?

_________ e. Why was Robert Thompson to assist Joseph?

_________ f. Why does the Lord love Hyrum Smith?

_________ g. Where were David Patten, Edward Partridge, and Joseph Smith, Senior?

_________ h. Why was George Miller to be trusted?

_________ i. Why was a house to be built?

________ j. When is the only time the Lord permits baptisms for the dead to be performed outside his temple?

________ k. Why are the Lord's people commanded to build temples?

________ l. What will the Lord do for those who follow his counsel diligently but are hindered by their enemies?

________ m. In verse 51, what obligation were the Saints released from? (See also D&C 115:8–11.)

________ n. How was the Nauvoo House to be paid for?

________ o. What did the Lord say concerning Vinson Knight?

________ p. What had the Lord prepared for the inhabitants of Kirtland?

________ q. What was Hyrum Smith to do?

________ r. What blessings were given to William Law?

________ s. Who were not allowed to buy stock in the Nauvoo House?

________ t. What was Joseph called to do?

________ u. Why was Joseph given two counselors?

________ v. What keys do the Twelve hold?

________ w. Why did the Lord provide these offices and their keys in his church?

Doctrine and Covenants 125

VERSE NUMBER

________ a. Where and when was the revelation recorded in Doctrine and Covenants 125 received?

________ b. How were the Saints to prepare for that which was to come?

_________ c. Where in Iowa was the city of Zarahemla to be built?

Doctrine and Covenants 126

VERSE NUMBER

_________ a. Where and when was the revelation recorded in Doctrine and Covenants 126 received?

_________ b. Why was Brigham Young not required to leave his family?

_________ c. Who was Brigham to take "especial care" of?

Doctrine and Covenants 127

VERSE NUMBER

_________ a. What is Doctrine and Covenants 127?

_________ b. Why did Joseph Smith leave Nauvoo?

_________ c. When did the Prophet Joseph intend to return?

_________ d. What would Joseph do to his enemies?

_________ e. What instructions did Joseph give concerning the temple?

_________ f. What instructions did Joseph give concerning baptism for the dead?

_________ g. What was Joseph's prayer to God?

Doctrine and Covenants 128

VERSE NUMBER

_________ a. What is Doctrine and Covenants 128?

_________ b. What had been on the Prophet's mind since he left?

_________ c. What was the recorder of the baptisms to do?

_________ d. Where is the book of life kept?

_________ e. Why is it important that ordinances be correctly recorded in the records of the Church?

_________ f. What "is in the likeness of the resurrection of the dead in coming forth out of their graves"?

_________ g. What is the baptismal font in similitude of?

_________ h. Whose salvation is necessary for our salvation?

_________ i. What is required for the earth to avoid being smitten with a curse?

_________ j. Who detected Satan when he appeared as an angel of light? (See v. 20*e*.)

_________ k. What book was to be presented to the Lord when his temple was finished?

Doctrine and Covenants 129

VERSE NUMBER

_________ a. What three grand keys are explained in Doctrine and Covenants 129?

_________ b. What are the two kinds of beings in heaven?

_________ c. What are we to do when a messenger comes with a message from God?

_________ d. What will the messenger do if he is an angel? A just man made perfect? A devil?

Why is it important for you to remember these keys?

Doctrine and Covenants 130

VERSE NUMBER

_________ a. Where and when was Doctrine and Covenants 130 received?

_________ b. What is the body of the Savior like?

________ c. What "will be coupled with eternal glory"?

________ d. Which angels minister to this earth?

________ e. What is the globe like where angels reside?

________ f. What will the earth be like in its immortal state?

________ g. What will be made manifest on it?

________ h. What will be made known by the white stone spoken of in Revelation 2:17?

________ i. To whom is the white stone given?

________ j. Where did the wars and destructions in the last days begin?

________ k. What will rise with us in the resurrection?

________ l. How is knowledge and intelligence to be obtained? (See also Bible Dictionary, p. 721, s.v. "Knowledge.")

________ m. What law is "irrevocably decreed in heaven"?

________ n. What kind of body do the Father and Son have? (See also Bible Dictionary, p. 681, s.v. "God.")

________ o. What kind of body does the Holy Ghost have? Why?

Doctrine and Covenants 131

VERSE NUMBER

________ a. Where and when was the revelation recorded in Doctrine and Covenants 131 received?

________ b. How many degrees are in the celestial glory?

________ c. How is the highest degree obtained?

________ d. In what kingdom can we have an increase?

________ e. What does the "more sure word of prophecy" mean?

________ f. In what condition is it impossible to be saved?

________ g. Why are we unable to see spirit matter now?

________ h. When will we be able to see it?

Doctrine and Covenants 132

VERSE NUMBER

________ a. What doctrines were revealed in the revelation recorded in Doctrine and Covenants 132 ?

________ b. What had Joseph Smith asked of the Lord?

________ c. Who must obey the Lord's law?

________ d. What is required for any agreement to be in effect for time and eternity?

________ e. What will become of those who are not married for time and eternity?

________ f. Why will those described in verse 19 be gods?

________ g. What is eternal life?

________ h. What will happen to those who are sealed but later apostasize, yet who do not shed innocent blood?

________ i. What is blasphemy against the Holy Ghost? (See also Alma 39:5–6.)

________ j. Why did Sarah give Hagar to Abraham?

________ k. Why are Abraham, Isaac, and Jacob gods?

________ l. What is required for Emma Smith to be forgiven?

________ m. Why may a man be given more than one wife?

Doctrine and Covenants 133

VERSE NUMBER

________ a. Where and when was the revelation recorded in Doctrine and Covenants 133 received?

________ b. Why had the Prophet inquired of the Lord?

________ c. Why were the Saints to be gathered out of Babylon?

________ d. What is spiritual Babylon?

________ e. What will the earth be like when the Lord comes?

________ f. Who will reign over all flesh?

________ g. Who are in the "north countries"? (See v. 26*a*.)

________ h. What will they do?

________ i. Who is the angel described in verse 36? (See Joseph Smith–History 1:33.)

________ j. What color will the Lord's garments be when he comes?

________ k. What will happen to the proud and the wicked at the Second Coming?

Doctrine and Covenants 134

VERSE NUMBER

________ a. What is Doctrine and Covenants 134?

________ b. Why are governments set up?

________ c. For what are we held accountable?

________ d. What three things must exist for a government to exist in peace?

________ e. To whom are we accountable for the way we worship?

________ f. How are punishments for various crimes to be determined?

_________ g. What are religious and other societies not to have power to deprive their members of?

Doctrine and Covenants 135

VERSE NUMBER

_________ a. Who wrote Doctrine and Covenants 135?

_________ b. Who killed Joseph and Hyrum Smith?

_________ c. What had the Prophet Joseph done?

_________ d. What had Joseph said before going to Carthage?

_________ e. What had Hyrum read before going to Carthage?

_________ f. How were they put in jail?

Doctrine and Covenants 136

VERSE NUMBER

_________ a. Where and when was the revelation recorded in Doctrine and Covenants 136 received? (See also Map, p. 298.)

_________ b. Who received this revelation?

_________ c. How were the Saints to be organized?

_________ d. Who were each company to take an equal number of? Why?

_________ e. What were the Saints to cease doing?

_________ f. What should be done with things that are borrowed and things that are found?

_________ g. How were the Saints to learn wisdom?

_________ h. Why was Joseph Smith killed?

_________ i. Why were the Saints to be diligent in keeping the commandments?

Doctrine and Covenants 137

VERSE NUMBER

_________ a. By whom and when was the revelation recorded in Doctrine and Covenants 137 received?

_________ b. Which glory did Joseph Smith see?

_________ c. Who did Joseph see in this vision? (Joseph's parents were still alive when this vision was received.)

_________ d. How was Alvin able to be in the celestial kingdom without being baptized?

_________ e. How does the Lord judge all men?

Doctrine and Covenants 138

VERSE NUMBER

_________ a. Who received the vision recorded in Doctrine and Covenants 138?

_________ b. What was President Joseph F. Smith doing when he was prompted to read 1 Peter 3 and 4?

_________ c. What happened as he "pondered over these things"?

_________ d. Who "were filled with joy and gladness"? Why?

_________ e. What did the Son of God do when he visited them?

_________ f. Where did Jesus not go?

_________ g. When did Christ minister to the dead?

_________ h. How did the Lord preach to those spirits in prison?

_________ i. What were these spirits taught?

_________ j. How did the dead look upon their long separation of body and spirit?

________ k. What individuals, who are named in verse 53, did President Smith see in the spirit world?

________ l. What did he observe about them?

________ m. What do the faithful elders do when they die?

________ n. How will the dead be redeemed?

________ o. When will they receive their reward?

Official Declaration–1

PARAGRAPH

________ a. Why was the Endowment House taken down?

________ b. Why did the Church stop the teaching of plural marriage and no longer permit "any person to enter into its practice"?

________ c. Who wrote Official Declaration–1?

________ d. What was the motion of President Lorenzo Snow?

________ e. How was his motion received by those attending general conference?

Excerpts

PARAGRAPH

________ a. To whom is it always safe to look for guidance and direction? Why?

________ b. What question did the Lord request President Wilford Woodruff to ask the members of the Church? Why?

________ c. Why did President Woodruff issue the Manifesto, stopping plural marriage?

Official Declaration–2

PARAGRAPH

________ a. When was the revelation recorded in Official Declaration–2 presented to the Church?

_________ b. Who received this revelation?

_________ c. To whom were the priesthood and temple blessings extended?

_________ d. What had led to the receipt of this revelation?

_________ e. How was the proposal to accept this revelation received by those attending general conference?

Joseph Smith–History

VERSE NUMBER

_________ a. Why did Joseph Smith write this history?

_________ b. What did Joseph present in his history?

_________ c. When and where was Joseph born? (See also map, page 295.)

_________ d. What caused "great confusion and bad feeling" among the priests and people?

_________ e. What scripture had a powerful effect on the heart of Joseph?

_________ f. What happened to Joseph when he began to pray?

_________ g. What did Joseph see as he was about to be destroyed?

_________ h. What did Joseph see and hear after the pillar of light fell upon him?

_________ i. What was the purpose of Joseph's prayer?

_________ j. Why was Joseph told he must join none of the churches?

_________ k. How did one of the Methodist preachers react to Joseph's account of his vision?

_________ l. What was not in Joseph's nature?

_________ m. What did Joseph have "full confidence in obtaining" on the evening of 21 September 1823?

_________ n. What did Moroni tell Joseph during his visits?

________ o. What was Joseph told when he received the plates?

________ p. How did Oliver Cowdery help Joseph?

________ q. What did Oliver and Joseph do immediately after being baptized? What effect did the Holy Ghost have upon their minds?

What wisdom would you like to receive from God? (See Joseph Smith–History 1:11.) What is required to obtain this wisdom?

Answers

Explanatory Introduction
a. paragraph 1
b. paragraph 1
c. paragraph 3
d. paragraph 4
e. paragraph 5
f. paragraph 6
g. paragraph 8
h. paragraph 8
i. paragraphs 10–11
j. paragraphs 12–13
k. paragraphs 14–15

Chronological Order of Contents
a. first page
b. first page
c. second page
d. second page
e. both pages

D&C 1
a. Headnote
b. Headnote
c. 1–2
d. 3
e. 4–5
f. 16
g. 17–23
h. 24–28
i. 33
j. 35–36
k. 37
l. 38

D&C 2
a. Joseph Smith–History 1:36–39
b. 1–2
c. 3

D&C 3
a. Headnote
b. 4
c. 8
d. 10–11
e. 12–15
f. 19–20

D&C 4
a. Headnote
b. 1
c. 2
d. 3
e. 5
f. 6–7

D&C 5
a. Headnote
b. 4
c. 6
d. 13
e. 19
f. 21–22
g. 24–25
h. 26
i. 28
j. 32–34

D&C 6
a. Headnote
b. 3
c. 7
d. 9
e. 8:2–5
f. 11–12
g. 14
h. 15–17
i. 18–19
j. 22–24
k. 25–28
l. 33–37

D&C 7
a. Headnote
b. Headnote
c. 3, 6
d. 5, 7

D&C 8
a. Headnote
b. 2–3
c. 4
d. 10
e. 11

D&C 9
a. Headnote
b. 1, 4
c. 7–8
d. 8–9
e. 13–14

D&C 10
a. Headnote
b. 1–2
c. 1
d. 6–7
e. 4
f. 5
g. 10–19
h. 22, 27
i. 24–27
j. 34–37
k. 38, 44
l. 46
m. 47–52
n. 56
o. 63
p. 69

D&C 11
a. Headnote
b. 5
c. 6–9
d. 12
e. 16–17
f. 20–27
g. 30

D&C 12
a. Headnote
b. 6–7
c. 8

D&C 13
a. Headnote
b. Headnote
c. Headnote
d. 1
e. 1

D&C 14
a. Headnote
b. Headnote
c. 7
d. 8
e. 8
f. 11

D&C 15
a. Headnote
b. Headnote
c. 4
d. 6

D&C 16
a. Headnote
b. Headnote
c. 4
d. 6

D&C 17
a. Headnote
b. 1
c. 2
d. 3–5
e. 6
f. 8

D&C 18
a. Headnote
b. 2
c. 3–5
d. 10
e. 13–16
f. 15–16
g. 23
h. 31–33
i. 37–38
j. 44

D&C 19
a. Headnote
b. Headnote
c. 2–3
d. 16
e. 15–18
f. 18
g. 27
h. 33
i. 35b
j. 38

D&C 20
a. Headnote
b. 1
c. Joseph Smith–History 1:33
d. 11–12
e. 14
f. 17–36
g. Moses 6:60
h. 37
i. 38–45
j. 46–52
k. 53–59
l. 65
m. 70
n. 71–74
o. 75
p. 77
q. 77
r. 79
s. 79

D&C 21
a. Headnote
b. 1
c. 3
d. 4–6
e. 7
f. 7–8
g. 9

D&C 22
a. Headnote
b. 4

D&C 23
a. Headnote
b. 1
c. 2
d. 3
e. 4
f. 5
g. 6–7

D&C 24
a. Headnote
b. 1
c. 5
d. 6
e. 8
f. 10–12
g. 18

D&C 25
a. Headnote, 1
b. 2
c. 5–7
d. 8
e. 11–12
f. 12
g. 15

D&C 26
a. D&C 24 headnote
b. 1
c. 2

D&C 27
a. Headnote
b. 2
c. 2
d. 5
e. 5–12
f. 11
g. 12
h. 15, 18
i. 16–18

D&C 28
a. Headnote
b. 2
c. 3
d. D&C 57:2–3
e. 11
f. 2 Nephi 32:5

D&C 29
a. Headnote
b. 2
c. 7
d. 8
e. 9
f. 11
g. 12
h. 13
i. 14–21
j. 22–28
k. 34–35
l. 39
m. 40
n. 41
o. 42–43
p. 44–45
q. 47

D&C 30
a. Headnote
b. 1–2
c. 4
d. 5–8
e. 5–6
f. 9–11

D&C 31
a. Headnote
b. 2, 6
c. 3, 7–8
d. 9
e. 11
f. 12

D&C 32
a. Headnote
b. 1–2
c. 4
d. 4

D&C 33
a. Headnote
b. 2
c. 4
d. 6
e. 10–11
f. 16

D&C 34
a. Headnote
b. 4–5
c. 7
d. 8–9
e. 10

D&C 35
a. Headnote
b. Headnote
c. 2
d. 6
e. 9
f. 12
g. 18
h. 20
i. 24

D&C 36
a. Headnote
b. 1
c. 2
d. 4–6

D&C 37
a. Headnote
b. 1
c. 2
d. 3a

D&C 38
a. Headnote
b. 2 Nephi 28:15
c. 8
d. 11–12
e. 20
f. 22
g. 24–25
h. 28–29
i. 30–31
j. 32
k. 35
l. 39
m. 40
n. 41

D&C 39
a. Headnote
b. 4
c. 6
d. 9
e. 10
f. D&C 95:8–9; 110:8–10

g. 18
h. 23

D&C 40
a. Headnote
b. 2
c. 2

D&C 41
a. Headnote
b. Headnote
c. 1
d. 2–3
e. 3
f. 5
g. 9
h. 11

D&C 42
a. Headnote
b. 3
c. 6–7
d. 11, 14
e. 14
f. 18–19, 79
g. 20–24
h. 27
i. 30–31
j. 33–35
k. 42
l. 46
m. 48
n. 71–73
o. 78
p. 79, 84–86
q. 88–89
r. 91

D&C 43
a. Headnote
b. Headnote
c. 2–5, 12
d. 6
e. 8–10
f. 12–13
g. 15
h. 16
i. 25
j. 33
k. 34

D&C 44
a. Headnote
b. 2
c. 4–5
d. 6

D&C 45
a. Headnote
b. 3–5
c. 9
d. 11–12
e. 17
f. 26–33
g. 29
h. 39
i. 40–43
j. 48–50
k. 52
l. 53
m. 54
n. 55
o. 57
p. 57–59
q. 65–67
r. 68
s. 70

D&C 46
a. Headnote
b. 3
c. 4
d. 7
e. 8
f. 9, 26
g. 13–25
h. 27
i. 33

D&C 47
a. Headnote
b. 1–3
c. 4

D&C 48
a. Headnote
b. 4
c. 6

D&C 49
a. Headnote
b. 1, 3
c. 1, 4
d. 11–14
e. 19
f. 20
g. 21
h. 24

D&C 50
a. Headnote
b. Headnote
c. 2–3
d. 5
e. 9
f. 14
g. 15
h. 17–18
i. 19–21
j. 22
k. 24
l. 26–28
m. 31–33
n. 40

D&C 51
a. Headnote
b. 3
c. 5
d. 8
e. 9
f. 13; D&C 83:6
g. 15
h. 19

D&C 52
a. Headnote
b. 3–5
c. 9–10
d. 13
e. 14
f. 14–19
g. 2, 33, 42
h. 34
i. 39
j. 40

D&C 53
a. Headnote
b. 1
c. 2–5
d. 7

D&C 54
a. Headnote
b. 3
c. 4–6
d. 7
e. 8

D&C 55
a. Headnote
b. 1–2
c. 2–4
d. 5

D&C 56
a. Headnote
b. 1–4
c. 7
d. 8–10
e. 14–15
f. 16
g. 17
h. 18

D&C 57
a. Headnote, 1
b. Headnote
c. Headnote
d. 3
e. 6, 8–10
f. 7
g. 11–12
h. 13
i. 15

D&C 58
a. Headnote
b. 3
c. 4
d. 6–13
e. 14–15
f. 16–18
g. 21–22
h. 26
i. 27
j. 28
k. 29–33
l. 42
m. 43
n. 60
o. 64

D&C 59
a. Headnote
b. Headnote
c. Headnote
d. 1–4
e. 5–6
f. 6–9
g. 9–15
h. 16–19
i. 21

D&C 60
a. Headnote
b. 2
c. 3
d. 5
e. 12–15

f. 15

D&C 61

a. Headnote
b. 2
c. 3
d. 15
e. 17
f. 18–24
g. 36–39

D&C 62

a. Headnote
b. 3
c. 4–5
d. 6

D&C 63

a. Headnote
b. Headnote
c. 6
d. 9
e. 10
f. 11
g. 16
h. 17–18
i. 23
j. 24
k. 28
l. 33
m. 41
n. 50–51
o. 55–56
p. 64

D&C 64

a. Headnote
b. 7
c. 8
d. 9
e. 10
f. 11
g. 12–14
h. 21–22
i. 23
j. 33–34
k. 41

D&C 65

a. Headnote
b. 2
c. 2
d. 3–5
e. 5–6

D&C 66

a. Headnote
b. 1–2
c. 3
d. 5–11
e. 12

D&C 67

a. Headnote
b. Headnote
c. 3
d. 5–7
e. 8–9
f. 10
g. 12–13

D&C 68

a. Headnote
b. 3–4
c. 4
d. 7–12
e. 15, 19–20
f. 16–18
g. 25–29
h. 27
i. 31

D&C 69

a. Headnote
b. 1–2
c. 3–4
d. 5
e. 7–8

D&C 70

a. Headnote
b. 3, 5
c. 4
d. 6–8
e. 12–13
f. 14–16

D&C 71

a. Headnote
b. 1
c. 4
d. 6
e. 7–10
f. 9–10

D&C 72

a. Headnote
b. 3
c. 4
d. 8
e. 10–11
f. 16–18, 25–26
g. 21–22
h. 24–26

D&C 73

a. Headnote
b. 1a
c. 3–4

D&C 74

a. Headnote
b. 3–4
c. 5–6

D&C 75

a. Headnote
b. 3–4
c. 5
d. 6–9, 17
e. 9–11
f. 13–14
g. 15
h. 19
i. 24–25
j. 29

D&C 76

a. Headnote
b. Headnote
c. 5–10
d. 12–13
e. 14
f. 22–27
g. 31–35
h. 33–39, 43–49
i. 51–60
j. 62–70
k. 71–75, 79
l. 77
m. 82–85, 101–110
n. 86, 88
o. 92
p. 94–95
q. 114–117

D&C 77

a. Headnote
b. Revelation 4 headnote
c. 1
d. 2
e. 4
f. 6
g. 7
h. Revelation 7 headnote
i. 8
j. 9
k. 10
l. 11
m. Revelation 8–9 headnotes
n. 12
o. 13
p. Revelation 10 headnote, 14
q. Revelation 11 headnote

D&C 78

a. Headnote
b. 3
c. 6
d. 7
e. 10
f. 11–15
g. D&C 27:11
h. 19

D&C 79

a. 1
b. 1
c. 2
d. 3

D&C 80

a. 1
b. 1, 3
c. 4

D&C 81

a. Headnote
b. 1
c. 2
d. 3–5
e. 6

D&C 82

a. Headnote
b. 1
c. 2
d. 3
e. 10
f. 12, 14–15
g. 19
h. 21
i. 22

D&C 83

a. Headnote
b. 2
c. 2

d. 4
e. 5–6

D&C 84
a. Headnote
b. 1
c. 3–4
d. 4–5
e. 6–16
f. 19
g. 20–22
h. 23
i. 26–27
j. 28
k. 33
l. 33–40
m. 44
n. 45
o. 44–47
p. 50–51
q. 54–55
r. 56–58
s. 65–72
t. 73
u. 77
v. 80–94
w. 97–98
x. 106
y. 109–110

D&C 85
a. Headnote
b. 1–2
c. 3
d. 9–11

D&C 86
a. Headnote
b. Matthew 13:13–43
c. 2
d. 2
e. 3
f. 5–6
g. 7

D&C 87
a. Headnote
b. 1
c. 4
d. D&C 109:65
e. 6
f. 8

D&C 88
a. Headnote
b. 1
c. 2
d. Bible Dictionary, p. 648, s.v. "Comforter"
e. 4
f. 15
g. 18–19
h. 20
i. 22
j. 27–29
k. 35
l. 49
m. 62
n. 65
o. 67–68
p. 69
q. 74–77
r. 78–80
s. 81–82
t. 87
u. 94–107
v. 95–98
w. 111–114
x. 118–126
y. 127

D&C 89
a. Headnote
b. Headnote
c. 2
d. 4
e. 7
f. 8
g. 9–11
h. 12–13
i. 18–21

D&C 90
a. Headnote
b. 5
c. 6–7
d. 10
e. 11
f. 13–18
g. 28–31
h. 34
i. 36

D&C 91
a. Headnote
b. 1–6
c. 4–6

D&C 92
a. Headnote
b. 1
c. 2

D&C 93
a. Headnote
b. 1
c. 6
d. 4, 14
e. 15
f. 19
g. 21, 23, 29
h. 24
i. 27
j. 28
k. 31–32
l. 36
m. 36–37
n. 39
o. 40
p. 49
q. 53

D&C 94
a. Headnote
b. 1
c. 3
d. 8–9
e. 10

D&C 95
a. Headnote
b. 1
c. 3–4, 8
d. 6
e. 8
f. 10
g. 11
h. 16
i. 17

D&C 96
a. Headnote
b. 5
c. 6
d. 8

D&C 97
a. Headnote
b. 1
c. 5
d. 8
e. 10–11
f. 12–14
g. 16
h. 18–19
i. Bible Dictionary, p. 792, s.v. "Zion"
j. 25, 27
k. 26

D&C 98
a. Headnote
b. Headnote
c. 2
d. 5–6
e. 9
f. 10
g. 12
h. 13–15
i. 21
j. 25–26
k. 27
l. 28–29
m. 32–33
n. 34–37
o. 41–44
p. 44

D&C 99
a. Headnote
b. 1
c. 2
d. 6

D&C 100
a. Headnote
b. 1
c. 3–4
d. 5
e. 5–6
f. 7
g. 8
h. 9
i. 10
j. 11
k. 16

D&C 101
a. Headnote
b. 1–2
c. 5
d. 6
e. 7–9
f. 21
g. 24–34
h. 35
i. 39
j. 41

k. 73
l. 77–80
m. 99

D&C 102

a. Headnote, 1
b. 2
c. 8
d. 15
e. 30–31

D&C 103

a. Headnote
b. 2–4
c. 5–7
d. 8–10
e. 12–13
f. 29
g. 30–34
h. 36

D&C 104

a. Headnote
b. 4
c. 4
d. 9
e. 10
f. 15–16
g. 17
h. 18
i. 51–52
j. 62
k. 67–69
l. 78–86

D&C 105

a. Headnote
b. Headnote
c. 2–4, 9
d. 5
e. 10–12
f. 19
g. 23–24, 38–41
h. 29–30
i. 37
j. 38–40

D&C 106

a. Headnote
b. 1
c. 2–3
d. 6

D&C 107

a. Headnote
b. 2–4
c. 8, 18–19
d. 11
e. 12
f. 14, 20
g. 22
h. 23, 33, 35
i. 25, 34
j. 27, 30
k. 31
l. 42–43
m. 48
n. 53–56
o. 71–74
p. 78–80
q. 85
r. 91–92
s. 99–100

D&C 108

a. Headnote
b. 1–2
c. 4
d. 7

D&C 109

a. Headnote
b. 4
c. 5
d. 13
e. 14–15
f. 16
g. 20
h. 22
i. 25–26
j. 38
k. 39
l. 50–53
m. 67
n. 68–70
o. 78

D&C 110

a. Headnote
b. Headnote
c. 2–3
d. 5
e. 6–7
f. 8
g. 11
h. 12
i. 13–16

D&C 111

a. Headnote
b. Headnote
c. 3
d. 5
e. 8

D&C 112

a. Headnote
b. 3
c. 4–12
d. 10
e. 1, 11
f. 14–15
g. 23–24
h. 25–26
i. 33
j. 34

D&C 113

a. Headnote
b. 2
c. 4
d. 6
e. 7–8
f. 10

D&C 114

a. Headnote
b. 1
c. 2

D&C 115

a. Headnote
b. Headnote, 1–3
c. 4
d. 6
e. 7
f. 8
g. 17

D&C 116

a. Headnote
b. 1

D&C 117

a. Headnote
b. 1–4
c. 8
d. 8
e. 11
f. 14

D&C 118

a. Headnote
b. 2
c. 3
d. 4
e. 6

D&C 119

a. Headnote
b. Headnote
c. 4
d. 6

D&C 120

a. Headnote
b. 1

D&C 121

a. Headnote
b. Headnote
c. 1–3
d. 4–6
e. 7–10
f. 17
g. 23–24
h. 26
i. 34–40
j. 36
k. 37
l. 39
m. 41–44
n. 43
o. 45–46

D&C 122

a. Headnote
b. 2
c. 7
d. 9

D&C 123

a. Headnote
b. 1–6
c. 6
d. 10
e. 12
f. 17

D&C 124

a. Headnote
b. Headnote
c. 2
d. 3
e. 12
f. 15
g. 19
h. 20
i. 22–24, 60
j. 30
k. 39–41
l. 49
m. 51

n. 63
o. 74–76
p. 83
q. 77, 91–96, 124
r. 97–101
s. 119–120
t. 125
u. 126
v. 128
w. 143

D&C 125

a. Headnote
b. 2
c. 3

D&C 126

a. Headnote
b. 1–3
c. 3

D&C 127

a. Headnote
b. 1
c. 1
d. 2
e. 4
f. 6
g. 12

D&C 128

a. Headnote
b. 1
c. 3–4
d. 7
e. 8
f. 12
g. 13
h. 15, 18
i. 17–18
j. 27:11
k. 24

D&C 129

a. Headnote
b. 1–3
c. 4
d. 5–8

D&C 130

a. Headnote
b. 1
c. 2
d. 5
e. 7–8
f. 9
g. 9
h. 10
i. 11
j. 12
k. 18
l. 19
m. 20–21
n. 22
o. 22

D&C 131

a. Headnote
b. 1
c. 2–3
d. 4
e. 5
f. 6
g. 7
h. 8

D&C 132

a. Headnote
b. 1
c. 3
d. 7
e. 15–17
f. 20
g. 24
h. 26
i. 27
j. 34–35
k. 37
l. 56
m. 63

D&C 133

a. Headnote
b. Headnote
c. 9
d. 14
e. 23–24
f. 25
g. D&C 110:11
h. 26–33
i. Joseph Smith–History 1:33
j. 48
k. 64–73

D&C 134

a. Headnote
b. 1
c. 1
d. 2
e. 4
f. 8
g. 10

D&C 135

a. Headnote
b. 1
c. 3
d. 4
e. 4–5
f. 7

D&C 136

a. Headnote
b. Headnote
c. 2–5
d. 8
e. 23–24
f. 25–26
g. 32–33
h. 39
i. 42

D&C 137

a. Headnote
b. 1
c. 3, 5, 10
d. 7
e. 9

D&C 138

a. Headnote
b. 1–6
c. 11
d. 12–18
e. 18–19
f. 20–22
g. 27
h. 30–32, 36–37
i. 31–35
j. 50
k. 53
l. 55–56
m. 57
n. 58
o. 59

Official Declaration–1

a. paragraph 3
b. paragraph 4
c. paragraph 5
d. paragraph 6
e. paragraph 6

Excerpts

a. paragraph 1
b. paragraph 4–6
c. paragraph 7

Official Declaration–2

a. paragraph 1
b. paragraph 1
c. paragraph 1
d. paragraph 1
e. last line

JS–H

a. 1
b. 2
c. 3
d. 6
e. 11–12
f. 15
g. 16
h. 17
i. 18
j. 19
k. 21
l. 28
m. 29
n. 33–46, 53–54
o. 59
p. 67
q. 71, 73
r. 73–74